THE COVER: Following the entry of Oklahoma into the Union in 1907, Congress in 1908 changed to a 46-star flag. This was the flag that Admiral Robert E. Peary said he had "nailed to the North Pole" in 1909.

THE LIFE HISTORY OF THE UNITED STATES

Volume 9: 1901-1917

THE PROGRESSIVE ERA

TIME
LIFE
BOOKS ®

THE LIFE HISTORY OF THE UNITED STATES

Consulting Editor, Henry F. Graff

Volume 9: 1901-1917

THE PROGRESSIVE ERA

by Ernest R. May

and the Editors of

TIME-LIFE BOOKS

TIME-LIFE BOOKS, NEW YORK

TIME-LIFE BOOKS

FOUNDER: Henry R. Luce 1898-1967

Editor-in-Chief: Hedley Donovan
Chairman of the Board: Andrew Heiskell
President: James R. Shepley
Vice Chairman: Roy E. Larsen

MANAGING EDITOR: Jerry Korn
Assistant Managing Editors: Ezra Bowen,
David Maness, Martin Mann, A. B. C. Whipple
Planning Director: Oliver E. Allen
Art Director: Sheldon Cotler
Chief of Research: Beatrice T. Dobie
Director of Photography: Melvin L. Scott
Senior Text Editors: Diana Hirsh, William Frankel
Assistant Planning Director: Carlotta Kerwin
Assistant Art Director: Arnold C. Holeywell
Assistant Chief of Research: Myra Mangan

PUBLISHER: Joan D. Manley
General Manager: John D. McSweeney
Business Manager: John Steven Maxwell
Sales Director: Carl G. Jaeger
Promotion Director: Paul R. Stewart
Public Relations Director: Nicholas Benton

THE LIFE HISTORY OF THE UNITED STATES
Editorial Staff for Volume 9
EDITOR: Sam Welles
Assistant Editor: Harold C. Field
Designers: Douglas R. Steinbauer, Frank Crump
Staff Writers: Peter Meyerson, Jon Swan,
Alfred Lansing, Harvey Loomis,
Edmund White, Jonathan Kastner
Chief Researcher: Clara E. Nicolai
Researchers: Lilla Zabriskie, Jacqueline Coates,
Evelyn Hauptman, Patricia Tolles,
Natalia Zunino, Malabar Brodeur, Mary-Jo Kline,
Joan Scafarello

EDITORIAL PRODUCTION
Production Editor: Douglas B. Graham
Assistant Production Editors:
Gennaro C. Esposito, Feliciano Madrid
Quality Director: Robert L. Young
Assistant Quality Director: James J. Cox
Associate: Serafino J. Cambareri
Copy Staff: Eleanore W. Karsten (chief),
Gail Weesner, Florence Keith, Pearl Sverdlin
Picture Department: Dolores A. Littles
Art Assistants: James D. Smith, Wayne R. Young
Traffic: Carmen McLellan

THE AUTHOR of Volume 9 in this series, Ernest R. May, who has concentrated on the study of 19th and 20th Century American foreign policy, is Professor of History at Harvard University. From 1969 to 1971 he was Dean of the College, and from 1971 to 1974 he was Director of the Institute of Politics at Harvard. He has received grants from the Guggenheim Foundation and the Social Science Research Council. During 1963 and 1964 Professor May was a fellow at the Center for Advanced Study in the Behavioral Sciences, Palo Alto, California. He is the author of, among other works, *American Imperialism: A Speculative Essay; Imperial Democracy: The Emergence of America as a Great Power; The World War and American Isolation, 1914-1917;* and *"Lessons" of the Past: The Use and Misuse of History in American Foreign Policy.*

THE CONSULTING EDITOR for this series, Henry F. Graff, is Professor of History at Columbia University in New York.

Valuable assistance in preparing this book was given by Roger Butterfield, who served as picture consultant; photographer Nina Leen; Editorial Production, Norman Airey; Library, Benjamin Lightman; Picture Collection, Doris O'Neil; Photographic Laboratory, George Karas; TIME-LIFE News Service, Murray J. Gart. Revisions Staff: Harold C. Field, Joan Chambers.

CONTENTS

1. LORDS OF CREATION

THE speed at which the United States grew during the 19th Century astonished observers in the older nations. The changes were not only in size but in kind. Farms and villages gave way to factories and cities. Thomas Jefferson's earlier America, where "every one may have land to labor for himself, if he chooses," disappeared. In its place by 1900 was a nation where fewer than four workers in 10 were in agriculture; four families in 10 lived in an urban area; and industry produced 31.9 per cent of the world's coal, 34.1 per cent of its iron and 36.7 per cent of its steel. With a population larger than that of any European country except Russia and with exports greater than the United Kingdom's, the United States was already the foremost industrial country of the world.

Changes of this magnitude inevitably strained the social structure underlying this industrial might. Most conspicuously, the businessman became the most important figure in society. The merchant, the factor, the banker had of course been important earlier. They had, however, wielded less power, touched fewer lives. The millionaires and multimillionaires of 1900 paid the wages of millions of workers and, indirectly as buyers, shippers or processors of timber, farm products and livestock, affected the livelihoods of most families in the country.

No income taxes subtracted from their enormous fortunes. No regulatory agencies effectively interfered with their methods of doing business. They

MODISHLY CLOTHED LADIES, painted by John Sloan, parade along Fifth Avenue in 1909, reflecting the lavish age when the American lords of industry reigned supreme.

were answerable only to their consciences, and these consciences were comfortably insulated; for even from the pulpit they heard social Darwinist slogans affirming that life was inherently a struggle, that the fit merited riches and that the unfit deserved exploitation and poverty.

A handful of private citizens—the very rich—wielded immense power, and this was perhaps the most striking fact about the United States at the beginning of the 20th Century. A corollary was the fact that other men wielded relatively less power. The industrial worker was practically impotent. So was the farmer, dependent now on machinery, on the great companies that bought his produce, on the railroads that carried it and on a marketing system in which prices were determined by bids and sales on gigantic commodity exchanges located in distant metropolitan centers. And the men who had once stood at the top of the social ladder—clergymen, lawyers, politicians—had slipped far down the rungs.

To describe the America of this time, one has to begin by identifying the rich and by describing the magnitude of their power. One must then go on to tell of other Americans, above all of those in the middle class, who launched a battle to humble the plutocracy, to uplift the poor and to make America a country of equality, opportunity and freedom. For it was these struggles and their forward-looking resolutions that made the years 1901-1917 the Progressive Era.

Straddling the United States in this newspaper cartoon entitled "New Colossus of Roads," railroad giant E. H. Harriman was fiercely competitive in business. In his private life, he was highly considerate. Once when his wife, the busy mother of six children, expressed a desire to see the midnight sun, he quickly granted her wish by taking her off to Siberia.

SOME of the very rich men were not much different from the rich of the past. Those who were merchants, like John Wanamaker of Philadelphia and Marshall Field of Chicago, merely did a bigger business than earlier storekeepers. The proprietors of the nine-county XIT ranch in the Texas Panhandle and the King family, who owned a million acres in the Rio Grande basin, were simply working on a larger scale than had plantation owners of the 18th and early 19th Centuries.

But some of the very rich had interests and power running far beyond their lands, their cities or even their states. In the Northwest, from Washington down into northern California, the two most powerful men were Frederick Weyerhaeuser and James J. Hill. Yet neither even lived in the region. They were neighbors in St. Paul, Minnesota.

Weyerhaeuser was a short, burly German who came to the United States in 1852 at the age of 17 and went to work in a brewery. After toiling in a railroad construction gang, he found a job in a sawmill, learned the trade, rose to be a manager and started his own business. Even-tempered, kindly in manner, speaking heavily accented English, he was taken, as one of his foremen said, for "just a good-natured old Dutchman." Actually he was as shrewd and tough a businessman as any in that predatory age. First he squeezed out nearly all his rivals in the lumber trade of the northern Mississippi valley. Then he set his eyes on Washington, Oregon and Idaho. Before long he held more than a million acres there. In 1913 his company owned 96 billion board feet of standing timber.

Jim Hill was Canadian by birth, a bearlike man in body and temper. He too had begun small, first clerking in a store, then for a riverboat line, afterward becoming a railroad agent. Finally he gained control of a small railroad and began to expand it, initially across Minnesota and up into Canada, then, naming it the Great Northern, he pushed his empire westward across the

Rockies. Unlike other transcontinental builders, Hill was a sound railroad man who looked to the long-term prospects of his property. When other roads went bankrupt during the Panic of 1893, his did not. Indeed, he was able to acquire the Northern Pacific and with it control of the whole transportation network of the Northwest. From the Great Lakes to Puget Sound, Hill was the lord of the country.

In the Southwest the pre-eminent baron was Edward H. Harriman. A clergyman's son, he had started business life as a runner in Wall Street and rocketed upward, owning a seat on the Stock Exchange at 22. Slight and shy, he looked like an eight-dollar-a-week bookkeeper. In fact he was one of the boldest and most imaginative speculators ever seen in the stock market.

Harriman decided to become a railroader in earnest. He spent some years rebuilding the weakened fortunes of the Illinois Central. After acquiring the near-bankrupt Union Pacific, he had an observation car hitched to the front of a special train and traveled from Omaha to the Pacific Coast, noting where there should be new rails, gentler grades and fewer curves. Then he sold off superfluous properties to obtain working capital and turned the UP into a paying line. In 1901 he added the Southern Pacific, which gave him control of the principal transport system between Kansas City and California. Though New York City remained his home, he was more powerful in the states where his lines ran than any local nabob.

So it was with others. The Armours, Swifts, Morrises and Cudahys of Chicago bought most of the livestock of the Middle West; the McCormicks and Deerings, also of Chicago, virtually monopolized the manufacture of farm machinery.

In the South, James Buchanan Duke for years controlled four fifths of all U.S. tobacco production. Duke had grown up in the North Carolina backwoods and had determined in his teens to be a success. When his father sent him to an academy in Roxboro he exclaimed, "Why those Quakers want to teach a fellow Latin and poetry and such like. . . . I ain't going to be a preacher or a lawyer. I am going to be a businessman and make my pile."

And he did. At 18 he was a partner in a tobacco firm. Foreseeing a boom in cigarettes, he concentrated his efforts on them and used every imaginable promotion tactic, including wholesale giveaways of cigarettes to newly arrived male immigrants, the use of premium coupons and sponsorship of sporting events to make his company foremost in the country. Before he was 35 he had created, in the American Tobacco Company, a combine that completely dominated the trade.

IT was only natural that the greatest concentration of magnates should be found in the more populous, more urban, more industrialized areas. Ohio had Mark Hanna and Tom L. Johnson, whose Cleveland street railway companies formed only a part of their financial holdings. Western Pennsylvania had the coke and steel kings, Henry Clay Frick and Andrew Carnegie.

From Philadelphia the firm of William Cramp & Sons lorded it over the nation's shipbuilding industry. That city also claimed two of the most spectacular promoters of transportation and utility companies, William L. Elkins and P.A.B. Widener. In New York the industrial nobility was too numerous to list here. To mention only a few: Meyer Guggenheim and his sons presided over the smelting industry of most of America; John W. (Bet-a-Million) Gates,

Nikola Tesla, a genius who sold his alternating-current patents to George Westinghouse for a million dollars, died almost penniless. He was a dreamer whose electrical innovations included the induction motor, the predecessor of neon lights and concepts of wireless that made Marconi famous.

Philip Danforth Armour, mogul of meat packing, made two million dollars by guessing correctly that the Civil War would end before other gamblers thought it would. Ruined traders were forced to pay him $40 a barrel for pork that Armour could buy for $18 when Union victories depressed the market.

Henry Ford was considered mad by his partners when he dreamed of making a thousand cars a day. But the dream was reality by 1914; the automobile's image as a "picture of arrogance and wealth, with all its independence and carelessness," had given way to the era of the Model T and new mobility.

a stock market gambler, directed a nationwide network of plants producing finished steel products; another speculator, Charles R. Flint, controlled most of the nation's rubber factories.

Even within this aristocracy, there were gradations. Combinations and consolidations among timber companies, railroads, farm machinery manufacturers and the like took more money than even a Weyerhaeuser, a Hill or a McCormick had in his own bank account. To secure the needed funds, financiers had to be called on for help; as part payment for their services the bankers often got some degree of control over the new companies. Gradually a small number of bankers in industry, mostly in New York, emerged as the elite of the elite.

Not everyone turned to New York for money. Samuel Insull of Chicago, a powerful man in the vigorous new electric-power industry, was one of the mavericks. A genuine Cockney, born within the sound of London's Bow Bells, Insull as a young man had emigrated to the United States, hoping to become Thomas Edison's secretary. Within a relatively short time he was an important executive in Edison's enterprises. When the Edison organization was merged by New York financial interests with its leading competitor to form the General Electric Company, Insull reluctantly accepted a vice presidency of the new concern. But he soon resigned and moved to Chicago, where he could run a company of his own. Ever after he insisted on raising funds either in Chicago or, if necessary, in London. He never relaxed his rule against giving any New York banker a seat on the boards of directors he controlled.

Another eccentric in New York financiers' eyes was Henry Ford. As a Michigan farm boy in the 1870s, Ford absorbed the agrarian distrust of bankers that remained with him all his life. He started experimenting with gasoline-engined horseless buggies while he was a mechanical engineer in Detroit. The Ford Motor Company was founded on $28,000 in cash raised among small businessmen who shared Ford's vision of city streets jammed with cars. In 1908 the Model T realized his dream of a light, cheap, mass-produced family automobile. By 1911 Ford's company was the largest single producer in the booming industry, and Ford dealerships were eagerly bid for. Ford set a high price on the franchises he granted: A dealer had to pay in advance for any cars ordered. The proceeds enabled Ford to finance his vast expansion entirely through cash receipts. Frustrated investment bankers fumed, but Ford continued to spurn them. Then, increasingly cranky and autocratic, he decided to buy out all his original partners and turn the giant company into a family-owned enterprise. To accomplish this, he finally had to borrow $75 million in 1919, to be repaid by April 1921. By putting pressure on his dealers, forcing them to buy every car sent them or forfeit their franchises, he managed to pay off his note in cash.

INSULL and Ford were exceptions, however. The majority of those creating or enlarging industries or transportation or utility systems had to go to New York City, for that was where the money was. National banks throughout the country, taking advantage of legislation dating from Civil War days, could deposit most of their funds in New York and still fulfill the requirements for cash reserves. The regional banks profited from the better money rates paid by New York commercial banks, and New York banks such as the National City and First National became the biggest in the country.

The city's life insurance companies also had huge assets. The three largest firms—the Equitable, the New York Life and the Mutual of New York—accumulated hundreds of millions in liquid funds through the use of conservative actuarial estimates and ruthless cancellation of policies if even a single payment was missed. Trust companies held similar sums. And great investment banks such as Kuhn, Loeb and Company, J. P. Morgan and others acted on behalf of individuals and corporations possessing billions available for investment.

The men who could dispose of these resources—the nobility of the financial aristocracy—fell into several groups, one of which was called "the Standard Oil crowd." John D. Rockefeller Sr. was already in semiretirement by 1896, but his brother William, Henry H. Rogers, Henry M. Flagler, John D. Archbold and other managers of Standard Oil remained very active. Since Standard was realizing profits of $40 million to $60 million a year from the petroleum business, the company was, as financial writer John Moody commented, "really a bank of the most gigantic character—a bank within an industry." Standard executed its extracurricular transactions primarily through James Stillman's National City Bank.

William Rockefeller was a man of few words. So was Stillman, a Texan who had started his business career as an accountant at the age of 18. Stillman said he liked William Rockefeller because they could sit together 15 minutes without speaking. Rogers, the real leader of the group, was a different man altogether. In one mood he is recalled as showing "such a kindly good-will in these eyes . . . that the man does not live who would not consider himself favored to be allowed to turn over . . . his pocket-book without receiving a receipt." At other times Rogers could become "a relentless, ravenous creature, pitiless as a shark."

Rogers, 60 at the turn of the century, had flourished during the oil industry's most cutthroat times, and he carried into high finance the methods

'GOLD RUSH' IS STARTED BY FORD'S $5 OFFER

Thousands of Men Seek Employment in Detroit Factory.

Will Distribute $10,000,000 in Semi-Monthly Bonuses.

No Employe to Receive Less Than Five Dollars a Day.

By 1914, the story goes, unfair distribution of profits was worrying Ford. In a turbulent meeting he proposed raising the daily minimum wage to $3.00, then $3.50 and finally $4.75. James Couzens, Ford's partner, snapped: "I dare you to make it five dollars!" Ford did, and astounded the nation.

Although Ford was hailed even by labor as "the man most responsible for social progress," his early assembly lines (left) later on came to symbolize an age in which men and machines became indistinguishable. Ford did not create the assembly-line idea, but he developed it to a remarkable perfection.

11

of the ruthless trade in which he had been apprenticed. Instead of waiting for investment opportunities he created them, putting together gas, street railway, mining and railroad combinations and using any and all devices to absorb or ruin competitors.

The second great financial faction in New York centered around the investment bank of Kuhn, Loeb and Company. At the beginning of the 20th Century, the head of the firm was Jacob H. Schiff, a small, wiry, blue-eyed man born in the ghetto of Frankfurt, Germany. He had built a solid reputation on successful flotations of railroad bonds. Among the individuals and companies whose funds he could tap were E. H. Harriman, George Westinghouse, the London financier Ernest Cassel and the directors of the powerful Pennsylvania Railroad. New York banks, including Stillman's National City, would often work with Schiff. He sat on the boards of several powerful trust companies and until 1905 he was a director of the rich Equitable Life Assurance Society.

In sharp contrast to Henry Rogers, Jacob Schiff was a methodical, deliberate and conservative man. As late as 1899 he expressed reservations about the soundness of any industrial securities as a form of investment. A saver of string and wrapping paper, a stickler for absolute promptness, Schiff examined propositions put to him in meticulous detail. Only when he was fully satisfied with the prospects for profit would he arrange a syndicate to participate in a bond or stock issue.

It followed from this cautious approach that Kuhn, Loeb would manage an issue only if guaranteed the power to see that the funds were used prudently. Always discreet, Schiff would never have used Rogers' words: "All meetings where I sit as director vote first and talk after I'm gone." But in practice Kuhn, Loeb financing usually meant Kuhn, Loeb control.

THE same rule was even more strictly enforced if the financing was done by the banking group headed by J. Pierpont Morgan. An autocrat to his boot soles, Morgan was the son of a noted investment banker; the younger Morgan had never had to make his own way. His social standing was impeccable; his mathematical talents were considerable. When he was a student at the University of Göttingen in Germany, his professor of mathematics held out the promise of an instructorship and told young Morgan that he would have a good chance of succeeding to the chair. Professor Ulrich was one of the leading mathematicians in Europe, so his offer should have been irresistible. But Morgan felt committed to returning to America.

In Wall Street Morgan progressed both because of his connections and his talent. He floated some of the largest railroad bond issues and, after the railroads ran into financial trouble in the Panic of 1893, arranged a number of reorganizations designed to rescue them.

By 1895 Morgan's standing was such that President Cleveland turned to him when the government needed an emergency loan of $65 million in gold. This was probably the only instance in which Morgan made an exception to his rule that, as a condition for his financial services, he retain a large voice in the future policy of any enterprise he financed. His list of accounts was resplendent. Among the railroads, the New York, New Haven and Hartford, the New York Central, the Erie, the Chesapeake & Ohio, the Southern, the Philadelphia & Reading, the Great Northern and the Northern Pacific came

Although this cartoon shows J. P. Morgan dominating a smilingly agreeable Theodore Roosevelt, the President bluntly attacked the trusts. In fact, his campaign to regulate their power was called a "drunken debauch" by one of Morgan's lieutenants. T. R. was not deterred by the fact that Morgan and other magnates had contributed $2.1 million to his campaign fund.

to be known as Morgan lines. General Electric, American Telephone & Telegraph and International Harvester became Morgan trusts. Even at the beginning of the century, the Morgan empire was regarded as probably greater in extent than either Kuhn, Loeb's or Standard Oil's.

In part this may have been simply because Morgan personally was more imposing than Schiff or even Rogers. In his middle years he had a disfigurement that, in another man, might have seemed comical: A skin disease, *acne rosacea*, had turned his nose into a huge red bulb. But Morgan possessed a counterbalancing feature in his imposing eyes. The photographer Edward Steichen compared Morgan's eyes with the headlight of an onrushing express train. Glaring out from under thick, dark eyebrows, they seemed able to subdue the strongest and brashest men. And, said J.P.'s son-in-law and biographer, Herbert L. Satterlee, Morgan's manner, as he performed so mundane a task as walking to his office, went with his eyes:

> He swung his arms as he walked and took no notice of anyone. He did not seem to see the throngs in the street, so intent was his mind on the thing that he was doing. Everyone knew him, and people made way for him, except some who were equally intent on their own affairs; and these he brushed aside. The thing that made his progress different from that of all the other people on the street was that he did not dodge, or walk in and out, or halt or slacken his pace. He simply barged along, as if he had been the only man going down the Nassau Street hill past the Subtreasury. He was the embodiment of power and purpose.

In larger part, of course, it was Morgan's accomplishments, capped by the creation of the United States Steel Corporation, that gave him his prestige and power. Long interested in the metal industry, he at first limited himself to smaller combinations—trusts for the manufacture of finished steel products such as pipe and bridgebeams. But once these were created Morgan began to think not only of merging the specialized groups but also of uniting with them steel mills that could supply raw material. The question was whether so vast an organization could be built despite opposition from Andrew Carnegie's company, then the leading producer of steel. With profits comparable to those of Standard Oil, Carnegie could, if he so decided, build his own finishing plants and give a Morgan combination deadly competition. As it happened, however, Carnegie was planning to retire and devote his remaining years to philanthropy.

AT a banquet in New York the president of the Carnegie company, Charles M. Schwab, indicated that a consolidation might be possible. During a subsequent conference Morgan questioned Schwab through all of one night about prospects for a single company that would mine iron, convert it into steel and manufacture finished products on a scale that would minimize costs and maximize output. Satisfied at last, Morgan said: "Well, if Andy wants to sell, I'll buy. Go and find his price."

When Schwab brought back a scrap of paper on which Carnegie had penciled the sum he wanted for his assets—reportedly $492 million—Morgan glanced at it and said, "I accept." Soon the final negotiations were completed, and the new United States Steel Corporation was capitalized at $1,402,000,-000—the first billion-dollar corporation and the largest industrial organization the world had ever seen. U.S. Steel was to control over half the nation's

Andrew Carnegie, of Scottish origin, spent the last 38 years of his long life giving away $350 million, hence this 1901 cartoon. His gifts ranged from a whopping $60 million for libraries to modest $5,000 annual pensions to the widows of Roosevelt and Cleveland. He even paid off claims honored by a bank that was bilked by a woman claiming to be his illegitimate daughter.

steel production, and Morgan and his associates were to be in command of it.

The awe that this feat inspired was suggested in a wry commentary by "Mr. Dooley," the fictional Irish barkeep created by the newspaper columnist Finley Peter Dunne:

> Pierpont Morgan calls in wan iv his office boys, th' prisidint iv a naytional bank an' says he, "James," he says, "take some change out iv th' damper an' r-run out an' buy Europe f'r me," he says. "I intind to re-organize it an' put it on a paying basis," he says. "Call up th' Czar an' th' Pope an' th' Sultan an' th' Impror Willum, an' tell thim we won't need their sarvices afther nex' week," he says. "Give thim a year's salary in advance. An', James," he says, "Ye betther put that r-red headed book-keeper near th' dure in charge iv th' continent. He doesn't seem to be doin' much," he says.

Panic-stricken lady speculators, overwhelmed by the crash of 1901, crowd around the quotation board in one of the many offices catering to women. Women investors were active on Wall Street long before they gained the vote. In fact, when the first brokerage office owned by a woman opened in 1869, it netted a phenomenal $750,000 profit during the first six weeks of business.

IN 1901 Morgan had a titanic battle with Schiff and Harriman. The Chicago, Burlington & Quincy Railroad had come onto the market. Harriman, who wanted access to Chicago for his Union Pacific, tried to buy the Burlington line, but Morgan and Hill outbid him and acquired it for the Northern Pacific. Angered by his setback, Harriman began considering ways to reverse this result. It occurred to him that since railroads were usually controlled through ownership of a minority of voting stock, it might be possible to buy sufficient shares on the open market to secure majority control of Hill's Northern Pacific and, consequently, the Burlington. Working quietly on this daring scheme, Harriman and Schiff had their agents purchase shares in large and small lots. Their camouflage was so successful that even associates and friends of Morgan sold some shares to Harriman.

Morgan himself was vacationing in Europe, completely unaware of the plot. Hill, however, became suspicious. Rushing from the West Coast to New York by special train, he found his fears confirmed. Harriman had a clear majority of preferred stock and needed only 40,000 shares of common to complete his coup. An urgent cable went off to Morgan at Aix-les-Bains in France. Morgan fired back an order to buy 150,000 shares of Northern Pacific common. Using all their resources, his partners located and bought the outstanding shares. Though it was a narrow squeak, Morgan kept control of the line.

One result of the furious buying by the Harriman and Morgan interests was a panic in Wall Street. Having no knowledge of what was going on, speculators had taken advantage of the rise in price to sell Northern Pacific short; that is, to sell shares they did not own in the hope of being able to purchase the stock later at a much lower price, deliver it and pocket the difference between the high price at which they sold and the low price at which they would deliver. As delivery date approached, the short sellers discovered to their horror not only that prices had not fallen, but that most certificates were locked up either in Harriman's vaults or Morgan's. Desperately offering to pay anything for shares, the short sellers pushed the price of common from $110 to $1000. Major brokerage houses faced ruin. But Morgan, after consulting with Schiff, saved them by arranging for speculators to pay $150 a share and thus take punishing losses but not be thrown into bankruptcy.

A second result of the Northern Pacific battle was an arrangement to keep any such incident from recurring. Morgan created the Northern Securities Company, capitalized at $400 million, to hold the stock of the Northern Pacific, the Great Northern and the Burlington. With its vast resources, Northern

Securities would presumably be safe from raids. Moreover, Morgan voluntarily gave Harriman representation on its board, thus ensuring that cooperation rather than competition should be the rule.

Morgan's triumph over Schiff and Harriman, coupled with his statesmanship in rescuing the speculators and setting up the Northern Securities Company, gave him a standing far above that of any other financier. He was to suffer occasional setbacks, to be sure. For example, when he attempted to create a merchant shipping trust, English public opinion rose in alarm at the idea of American control over the sea lanes, and Morgan found himself unable to buy sufficient shipping to give him a commanding position on the Atlantic sea lanes. Morgan's International Mercantile Marine Company staggered along, beset by competition and depression. In 1914 the company had to suspend payment of interest on its obligations. But such episodes had little effect on his reputation as probably the most powerful man in America.

Morgan was the embodiment of a new order of men brought into being by industrialization. He was not himself an industrialist. Indeed, he may never have seen the inside of a factory. But neither was he a stock jobber like "Uncle Daniel" Drew or Jay Gould. When Morgan promoted a bond or stock issue, he naturally took a commission, often a big one. As a rule he and his partners and associates would get part of a new offering at a bargain price. Later they were able to sell their holdings at a profit. It was this fact that made other financiers eager to share in any undertaking that Morgan managed. And his firm frequently had inside information that enabled it to predict rises and falls in the prices of other stocks—with resulting gains.

Nevertheless the mere piling up of money was never of major concern to Morgan. Nearly everything he did was aimed at curbing the industrial and financial freebooting of men like Rockefeller, Carnegie, Drew and Gould. He sought to unify industries and transportation systems so that there would be no dog-eat-dog competition. When asked at a congressional hearing whether he favored combination or competition, he answered, "I would rather have combination." When pressed, he added, "I do not object to competition either. I like a little competition."

During the same hearing he was asked by committee counsel Samuel Untermyer about his motive in promoting great industrial consolidations. Morgan replied: "If it is good business for the interests of the country to do it, I do it." Untermyer then asked, "Is not a man likely, quite subconsciously, to imagine that things are for the interests of the country when they are good business?" Morgan gave a flat no.

Once more the lawyer tried to corner the financier, asking: "You think that you are able to justly and impartially differentiate, where your own interests are concerned, just as clearly as though you had no interest at stake, do you?" And J. P., using the minimum number of words consonant with courtesy, ended the discussion by saying, "Exactly, sir."

MORGAN'S guiding principles were that the interests of the nation and of the investing public were identical, that all businesses should be operated with primary regard for stockholders as a community, that control should be vested in men of character and that he, better than anyone else, could judge character. The results seemed to justify him. His influence and power grew.

In 1907 his strength was put to an exacting test, for in that year the boom

Morgan's self-consciousness about his huge, acne-ridden nose made him extremely camera-shy and, as shown here, he occasionally lashed out at news-hungry photographers. A popular Morgan legend relates that even his close friends and associates were prone to a dangerous self-consciousness: At a tea a partner's wife fluttered: "Mr. Morgan, do you take nose in your tea?"

that had continued ever since 1897 suddenly ended, and the financial community experienced a nerve-racking panic. Superficially the cause was easy to pinpoint. Frederick A. Heinze, an ingenious and unscrupulous engineer, had come East with the booty from Montana copper operations. He bought control of a bank, the Mercantile National, and used its assets to back up his stock speculations. When one of his bigger gambles failed, questions inevitably rose about the soundness of his bank. Worried depositors rushed to withdraw funds, and there were runs on other banks. Soon a number of trust companies were in danger. One of the largest, the Knickerbocker Trust, ran out of cash and, refused loans by other banks, had to close its doors. Although their situation was hardly better, the officers of other trust companies refused to ask for help, fearing that disclosure might further weaken their position.

The news of the deepening crisis had been relayed to Morgan, who was attending an Episcopal church convention in the South. To avoid a panic, Morgan waited until the convention was over, and then sped back to New York. He put experts to work assessing the strengths and weaknesses of the institutions in greatest danger. One of these, the Trust Company of America, seemed certain to go under. Rumors had connected some of its officers with Heinze. Moreover, an important financier had made insinuations about its strength to newspaper reporters. Just as the threatened bank's reserves were about to give out, Morgan learned that the company was fundamentally sound. He declared, "This, then, is the place to stop this trouble."

The presidents of the principal commercial banks were at the Morgan offices at the time. Morgan immediately organized a syndicate to lend money to the Trust Company. The lines outside the doors continued to grow. Each day more cash was required. Some was supplied by national banks, some by other trust companies, some by the United States Treasury which, at Morgan's urging, poured deposits into New York. At times it appeared that not enough could be raised. But Morgan always found a way. In the end the Trust Company and the rest of the New York banks were saved.

OTHER crises arose. The stock exchange tottered. Securities were being offered for sale, but those who wanted to buy them could not borrow the money with which to do so. Early one afternoon the president of the Stock Exchange told Morgan that the market would have to be closed. Morgan replied: "At what time do you usually close it?" "Why, at 3 o'clock," was the answer. In his usual brusque fashion, Morgan stated: "It must not close one minute before that hour today!"

Morgan called the principal bankers to meet with him at 2 o'clock. Within 16 minutes after the conference began, he sent word to the floor of the exchange that the House of Morgan had arranged for a $25 million fund to finance security purchases. Meanwhile, according to the New York *Tribune*, Morgan served notice on the big speculators that if they did anything during the crisis to depress stock prices "he would crush them."

On the days that followed, more money was needed to keep the exchange going and Morgan convinced banks or others to put it up. The exchange kept its regular hours, and while prices declined, they never broke in a wholesale slump. At the same time Morgan was dealing with other threats. He saved the credit of the City of New York. It had bonds falling due, and no one seemed ready to lend it new money. City officials turned in consternation to Morgan,

Napoleon saw China's potential might when he called it "a vast slumbering lion." In a cartoon dated a century later, Uncle Sam asks: "How long would this giant submit to being led around by little Europe?" But at that moment the U.S. was in vigorous competition with European business interests in Asia, which "belongs to us and we should control it," said Jim Hill.

and the financier organized a bankers' syndicate to raise the necessary funds.

At another point he rescued a major brokerage firm that seemed headed for disaster because its money was tied up in stocks for which there was no ready market. In exchange for its holdings he supplied U.S. Steel shares which were as good as cash. Had this firm failed, the ensuing crisis might well have brought down other large brokerage houses.

At every moment Morgan was general-in-chief. The Standard Oil crowd, Harriman, the heads of all the banks, the Secretary of the Treasury—everyone looked to him for leadership, and he gave it. Nothing that Morgan did was altruistic. In the end he stood to make large sums on the money lent. But he showed decisiveness and courage when others did not, and as a result, the shock of the Panic of 1907 was cushioned.

After it was over, there was no longer any doubt that Morgan stood in first place. William Rockefeller, Henry Rogers and others had lost large sums. The National City Bank, like the First National and the Chemical National, began to take its lead from Morgan. Thomas Fortune Ryan sold him control of the Equitable Life Assurance Society.

In 1912 Congress' Pujo Committee, investigating the question of whether or not there was a money trust, learned that Morgan, his partners and the directors of the major New York banks associated with them held 341 directorships in 112 corporations with aggregate resources of over $22 billion. Morgan's position as the pre-eminent American financier was unquestioned.

While there were other men who had larger personal fortunes, none approached J. P. Morgan in power, and none could rival his regal way of life. He kept a great house on Madison Avenue, an estate on the Hudson, a residence in London, a manor on the outskirts of that city and a succession of ocean-going yachts, each designed to be the most magnificent afloat and all of them flamboyantly named *Corsair*. When he traveled on land it was by special car or sometimes special train, for which the tracks ahead had been cleared. He spent several months of each year vacationing in Europe, always living in the highest style, often exchanging visits with royalty. But other Americans also had their palaces and yachts and private cars. To many it seemed as if America had suddenly sprouted a plutocracy as rich, as powerful and as arrogant as any that Europe had known.

Had they been better students of history, these princes of industry might have walked the earth with less confidence, for extremes of wealth and privilege had always begotten angry protest. Most recently, agrarian Populists and free silverites had scored brief and localized triumphs in the 1890s. While they had failed to muster the strength needed for victory on the national scale, within a few years they would be joined by others. Large numbers of middle-class city dwellers would find their privileges and position dangerously threatened. The Progressive movement—a new and far more effective coalition than the Populists—would appear, and it would be bound together by a common fear and resentment of the plutocracy.

At the beginning of the new century, America's prideful millionaires seemed the acknowledged lords of creation. The voices of reform sounded only distantly and with scant force as they exhorted the nation to turn toward progressive goals. But sooner than they could know, the plutocrats would find their power challenged on every hand.

Stern-faced John D. Rockefeller is satirized as the "King of Combinations," his crown girdled by his interests. This modern monarch stands on a storage tank of Standard Oil, the first big trust and the cornerstone of his empire. Rockefeller, like others among the money aristocracy, was able to trace a blood link to royalty—in his case to Henry I, King of France.

QUIETLY SKETCHING, Robert Henri (*left*) and John Sloan work as Henri's wife reads aloud and Dolly Sloan listens. This etching by Sloan celebrates his long, close friendship with Henri, his teacher and leader of the avant-garde Ashcan School.

A city's life in vivid portraits

THE opening years of the 20th Century were boom years for American cities. Filled with office and factory workers, shopkeepers and immigrants, cities bulged and spread. By legislation, New York City in 1898 had absorbed surrounding areas to become Greater New York—three times as vast and almost twice as populous as "little old New York" had been. To speed the daily travel of millions, armies of workmen dug tunnels in the earth, flung bridges across the encircling waters and erected massive railroad terminals.

The city's vigor and variety attracted a band of artists who were to revolutionize American art. These men were "The Eight"—Arthur Davies, William Glackens, Robert Henri, Ernest Lawson, George Luks, Maurice Prendergast, Everett Shinn and John Sloan. Their group exhibition in New York in 1908 both shocked and educated contemporary taste. Spurning the safe road of genteel society portraiture, The Eight painted men and machines at work, women at leisure. In time their brand of personalized realism earned them the nickname "The Ashcan School." Robert Henri, who had taught four of The Eight, insisted that artists should "make pictures from life," and the city life these artists saw was not fixed in one stiff pose. It was, by turns, rough and tender, somber and jubilant. For to them the city was, as John Sloan said, "a cosmopolitan palette where the spectrum changed in every side street."

SNOWY BACK YARDS are portrayed by Everett Shinn. Critics attacked his "vulgar point of view"; he attacked popular art as "merely an adjunct of plush and cut-glass."

RELAXING on a rooftop, women *(above)* dry their hair. This Sloan canvas, entered in the 1913 Armory Show, was admired by Theodore Roosevelt, but he did not buy it. Sloan did not sell any of his paintings until he was over 40 years old.

CELEBRATING on election night, crowds *(right)* blow noisemakers and scatter confetti as an elevated train thunders overhead. Sloan, who painted this scene, ran for the assembly as a Socialist in 1908 and was, he admitted, "glad to lose."

DANCING in the street, children *(left)* display the glow of life that delighted George Luks. A powerful man who claimed to be "the best barroom fighter in America," Luks especially enjoyed painting in New York's brawling Lower East Side.

Rooftop relaxation and
fun in crowded city streets

"FORGET about art," Robert Henri told his classes, "and paint pictures of what interests you in life." Henri's best students did not forget about art, but they did portray life with a new boldness and vision. For their subject matter they took to the streets. John Sloan preferred gamy sections like the Tenderloin to the elegant parts of New York. He enjoyed "the drab, shabby, happy, sad and human" life he found there.

The group's preference for ordinary people and commonplace settings came only partly from Henri's teaching. For Glackens, Luks, Shinn and Sloan it also came from their training as newspaper artists. Rapidly and accurately they had sketched the news of the day: murders, fires and parades. As painters they retained their eye for the immediate scene. Detesting false charm, they expressed the moods and caught the excitement of the city as no American artists had done before them.

The variety and vigor of a city's amusements

PAINTERS found a great variety of entertainment beckoning them in New York. Early in the 20th Century, there were dozens of "amusement resorts" on the Bowery alone: music halls, dance halls, concert-saloons and nickel movie houses. Of these Bowery resorts, the police classified very few as "respectable."

New York's respectable entertainments flourished farther uptown. Broadway theaters offered romantic comedies and melodramas—*The Rose of the Rancho, Julie Bonbon, Barbara's Millions.* For wittier fare producers were importing the plays of George Bernard Shaw. Caruso sang and Isadora Duncan danced in those days.

At Oscar Hammerstein's Victoria, a "theatre of varieties," Houdini did his magic and young Charlie Chaplin clowned. Atop the Victoria was Hammerstein's famous Paradise Roof Garden *(above, right)*. It was here that Hammerstein, armed only with a siphon of soda water, squirted a loose bear back into its cage.

Artists moved easily in this flamboyant world. In Greenwich Village Everett Shinn founded an acting company, wrote his own farces and, assisted by the Glackenses, staged them. Years later John Sloan said of those good times, "You young people don't realize how sweet—and sad—New York was before Prohibition."

GRACEFUL WIREWALKERS perform in Glackens' painting of a popular summer spot, Hammerstein's Roof Garden. The Garden had variety acts, singing waiters and a trained monkey.

GLIDING SKATERS turn and tumble (above) in this canvas by Glackens. Fond of sports, he also painted racetrack and sailing scenes. But when he went skating with Henri, he returned home expecting to be "black and blue in the morning."

WRITHING WRESTLERS grapple in this painting by George Luks. Luks, disgusted with the prim nudes that were fashionable in his time, set out to show "those pink and white idiots" of the National Academy what anatomy really looked like.

Landmarks
in changing
neighborhoods

McSorley's Old Ale House on East
Seventh Street opened for business
in 1854. Its founder's motto was:
"Good ale, raw onions, and no ladies." John Sloan, who called Mc-
Sorley's "the old standby," painted
five pictures of the place. In this
particular version the proprietor,
Old Bill McSorley, is feeding his
cats. He once had 18 of them.

According to Sloan, McSorley's
firm house rule against women and
mixed drinks kept the bar a "tem-
ple of temperance." Talk was free
and easy, though usually decorous.
Workers, businessmen, politicians,
artists, even an occasional anarchist felt at home here. In that city of
transients, saloons like McSorley's
brightened the streets and preserved a sense of neighborhood.

24

Excursions to the beach

As cities grew, more and more people vacationed at nearby resorts, and during the hot months beaches were crowded. Seaside outings had been a new craze in the 1850s; by the early 20th Century they were an established summer custom. People on holiday, in parks or at the shore, were a favorite subject

of artist Maurice Prendergast. His painting below shows swimmers and strollers at pebbly Revere Beach northeast of Boston.

Prendergast, who lived in and around Boston before he moved to New York in 1914, was shy, deaf and chronically poor. He eked out a meager living by carving picture frames and painting show cards. But in his own art he was the boldest of The Eight. Using techniques adapted from the French Impressionists, he created work which one critic called "an explosion in a color factory." His sunny colors and his flat, formal figures have exerted a continuing influence on American art.

A MISTY TRIP across the Hudson River to New Jersey is captured in John Sloan's *The Wake of the Ferry*. The artist observed that "optimistic people go to the front of the boat; the depressed stand in the stern."

STEAM ENGINES on surface tracks *(below)* in Lawson's *Old Grand Central* place the scene in time. By 1907 most of the trains entering this terminal were electric powered, and by 1913 all trains were arriving inside tunnels 40 feet underground.

A GREAT SPAN linking Manhattan with Queens, the Queensborough Bridge is boldly portrayed in Ernest Lawson's painting. The bridge, opened in 1909, helped triple Queens's population in less than 20 years.

An expanding city bound together

IN the early 1900s Greater New York was building energetically to unite its island center, Manhattan, with its outlying regions. Three new bridges were built between 1903 and 1910, and tunnels were constructed beneath the Hudson and the East Rivers. Subways began to carry passengers in 1904, and in 1907 New York's cab service was improved by the arrival of the first "taximeter" cabs—65 shiny red cars from Paris. With auto

traffic swelling, policemen were now posted to direct it.

Most artists turned away from the quickened, uglier scene before them, but the so-called Ashcan painters looked directly at it. They painted "city landscapes." They captured the city as its many distinct localities merged into one sprawling metropolis. Yet it was the smaller, slower city that they preferred. As Sloan said: "Who'd want to paint a street strewn with automobiles?"

2. THE OTHER HALF

ALMOST until the end of the 19th Century, the myth persisted that there were no poor in America or at least that the poverty-stricken could only blame their plight on their own failings—usually categorized as laziness or drunkenness. A corollary to this bit of mythology was the theory that anyone dissatisfied with his lot could pick up stakes, go west, cut a farm out of the wilderness and make a decent living. But in a celebrated paper delivered in 1893, historian Frederick Jackson Turner pointed out that the continuous line of frontier land had disappeared. Moreover, other research proved that while there was a continuing supply of free land, it was primarily taken up by farmers and not by industrial workers.

The American work force at the turn of the century numbered some 30 million men and women, nearly 11 million of whom were in agriculture. The rest included miners, lumberjacks, factory workers, seamstresses and domestic servants. By and large, all were poorly paid, and work was not always to be found. Though schedules varied from industry to industry, the average work week was 59 hours; the average rate of pay, taking account of skilled as well as unskilled workers, was less than $10 a week. In the steel industry an 84-hour week was not unheard of. In textile mills new hands frequently received 75 cents for a 10-hour day. And in many industries the practice was to produce full-blast at some seasons and shut down altogether at others, thus leaving the workers for long periods with no pay at all.

POVERTY IN AMERICA early in the 20th Century is depicted by George Bellows. Such slums, which bred crime and disease, also gave impetus to overdue social reforms.

Of the 4.5 million industrial workers, more than half a million were in the textile mills. Standard rates for the unskilled were less than 10 cents an hour; the customary work week was 62 hours; and, since the mills usually ran only nine months a year, the pay for even an experienced worker seldom exceeded $450 a year.

The garment industry was another huge employer of labor. It was concentrated in large cities, and it turned out work clothes and ready-to-wear. Fierce competition kept clothing prices low, and manufacturers tried to pay as little as possible for labor. Some manufacturers made entire garments. Others hired only cutters and finishers, sending pieces of fabric out to subcontractors to be made into sleeves, collars, trousers, and the like. These subcontractors in turn relied on their families for labor or had shops hidden away in attics or basements, where rent was a negligible expense.

Wages in garment factories varied from eight cents an hour for female pressers up to more than 25 cents for male cutters. On the average, a "learner" earned three to four dollars a week, the old hand about $14. But the factories generally were busy for only half the year—three months in the summer and three in the winter—standing practically idle in between. Small contractors paid by the piece rather than by the hour, and workers were pressed to speed their work. The nickname for such shops—"sweatshop"—is self-explanatory. At the piece rates paid, workers rarely could count on more than $200 a year. Evidence collected by social workers proved that sweatshop employees were more subject than other groups to tuberculosis and other diseases.

A child laborer stands at a spinning frame in a Southern mill in the early 1900s. By then some 1.5 million U.S. workers were under 16 years old, and they toiled up to 13 hours a day for a pittance. To improve their lot, Senator William E. Borah of Idaho introduced a bill that sought "to have the government do for children what it has already done for calves and pigs."

COAL miners, who numbered more than 344,000 in 1900, lived in remote communities where the company was frequently the only employer, landlord and storekeeper. The miners' workday began at dawn when they went down the shaft to the coal face. With picks or explosives or, more rarely, pneumatic drills, they pried chunks from the seam and shoveled them into ore cars. Pay was figured not by the hour but by the ton, not infrequently on the basis of a 2,700-pound or even a 3,360-pound "miner's ton."

Until he heard the whistle in the morning, the miner never knew whether he would have work or not, for when the price for coal dropped, companies cut back to a few days' operation a week. An average miner earned about $400 a year. To make ends meet, some miners' wives took in washing or did housework for foremen and managers. In anthracite mines, child workers picked out slate and rock.

Mill work, garment sewing and coal mining were only three among hundreds of occupations but, in working conditions and pay, they were more or less typical of industrial conditions in the early 1900s. Young single men could get by, for even $200 a year would leave some loose change to save or spend frivolously. But the man with a family, the widow or the worker with parents to support lived at best on the ragged edge of poverty.

Thoughtful observers were appalled by these conditions and wrote fact-filled books about the life of the industrial worker. In 1890 Jacob Riis had described the miserable situation of New York's working people in his book *How the Other Half Lives*. In *The Tenement House Problem* a corporation lawyer, Robert W. De Forest, statistically documented the horrors that Riis sketched —for example, tuberculosis rates of 38 per cent. Peter Roberts, a sociologist, described in exhaustive detail conditions in the anthracite coal communities.

Social workers like Lillian Wald in New York and Jane Addams in Chicago told of the misery they had seen in tenement districts.

In *The Workers*, published just before the new century, Walter Wyckoff described at first hand labor conditions in various parts of the country. Recently graduated from college at Princeton, he had set out in an old suit, with a pack on his back and nothing in his pockets, to find out what life was like among workers. In farming country he did odd jobs in return for board, lodging and 75 cents a day. Elsewhere he joined gangs of construction workers and loggers. In Chicago he worked at times in a factory, at others he was unemployed. With a friend, a jobless ironworker, he carried bags at a railroad station; when it snowed he shoveled sidewalks; and, when penniless, went to a police station to huddle on a cell floor with other vagrants, many of whom were covered with lice.

Wyckoff's writings tell mostly of pinched living, exhausting 12-hour workdays and so narrow a margin between income and outlay that holidays such as Christmas and New Year's were occasions for resentment because they meant no work and no pay. To Wyckoff the most distressing discovery was how low wages, coupled with the ever-present threat of layoff or illness, created a feeling of being a "superfluous human being."

In *The Woman Who Toils*, Marie and Bessie Van Vorst added further details to the picture drawn by Wyckoff. These two young women from a well-to-do family disguised themselves and went to work. Although never suffering real privation, they were often numbed by 10- and 12-hour days of piecework for which they earned barely a dollar. They saw children of eight and 10 working these same hours, girls bent and prematurely aged, boarding houses where life was animal-like. The Van Vorsts, like Wyckoff, could not, despite their earnestness, comprehend the endless vistas of workingmen's misery, for when their study was over they returned to warm beds, good food, handsome houses and trained servants. Nonetheless, their experience gave them insight into the awful insecurity that was part of the worker's life.

In 1904, in a book entitled *Poverty*, Robert Hunter added up the meager statistical data in existence and estimated that in 1900 at least 10 million of America's 76 million people were so poor they could not "obtain *those necessaries which will permit them to maintain a state of physical efficiency.*" Clinging to the old notion of America as a land of limitless opportunity, many reviewers found his figure incredible. Within two years, however, John A. Ryan, an economist, concluded that 60 per cent of the adult male workers earned too little to maintain a family. Although this meant that as many as 50 million Americans could be classified as poor, the evidence was now too clear to be denied. While industrialism had made a few hundred families fantastically rich, it had reduced millions of Americans to a state in which, as Hunter wrote, they lacked "a sanitary dwelling and sufficient food and clothing to keep the body in working order"—the "standard that a man would demand for his horses or slaves."

IN retrospect it may seem puzzling that these millions of downtrodden poor did not unite to do political battle with the wealthy and privileged. In Europe disciples of Karl Marx had had marked success in organizing socialist parties among workingmen and in securing reform legislation. Because 1900 to 1914 were the years of tremendous immigration from Southern and Eastern

In 1903 Marie and Bessie Van Vorst published a grim exposé of working conditions in factories. This report hastened the abolition of child labor in Southern mills and launched Marie on a prolific writing career. But as the author of some 40 novels, she admitted, "I have never written the things I wanted to write. I wrote coldly for money, without interest."

Europe, numbers of newcomers were at least somewhat familiar with socialism. Most of the more than 10 million immigrants in America by 1910 held the worst of jobs, with the longest hours and the lowest rates of pay, largely because few had a trade, fewer a command of English. The situation seemed ideally suited for a working-class political movement, especially since average American-born workers existed under similarly dismal conditions.

Around the turn of the century, when the trusts were reaching their height, some followers of Marxism and other left-wing philosophies actually did unite in a Socialist party. Earlier American socialist groups had been clannish, doctrinaire and largely ineffectual, but the Socialist party brought together such diverse elements as the East Europeans of New York, led by Russian-born Morris Hillquit, a successful lawyer; Wisconsin Germans led by Victor Berger, a schoolteacher of Austrian birth who had the instincts of a machine politician; an evangelist of socialism like Kate Richards O'Hare of Kansas; and the tough Western Federation of Miners led by the one-eyed giant, "Big Bill" Haywood.

Union leader "Big Bill" Haywood, accused of urging labor to use violence against capitalism, was tried for murder in Idaho in 1907. There was angry talk of lynching him. But his famous lawyer (opposite page) was determined that Haywood receive full justice under the system he sought to smash.

THE Socialist party attracted men of varied talents and backgrounds, including writers like Upton Sinclair and Jack London, clergymen and scholars. There were also mavericks from millionaire families like J. G. Phelps Stokes of New York, president of the Nevada Central Railroad; publisher and stock-promoter Gaylord Wilshire; and Joseph Patterson, later to be the owner-founder of the New York *Daily News*. Above all, the party had a national leader—Eugene V. Debs, onetime leader in the American Railway Union, veteran of the Pullman strike and a spellbinding orator. This son of a small-town Hoosier grocer radiated a simplicity and sincerity, almost a saintliness, that attached the whole party to him and helped keep it together.

In 1900, before the united party existed, Debs polled 87,814 votes as the Social Democratic candidate for President. As the Socialist candidate he ran up 402,283 in 1904, 420,793 in 1908 and more than 900,000 in 1912. Socialists meanwhile were winning control of local governments: 33 cities and towns, including Milwaukee, Wisconsin, Butte, Montana, and Flint, Michigan, had socialist administrations in the second decade of the century. Two Socialists, Berger of Milwaukee and Meyer London of New York, were congressmen.

Nor was Socialist influence and strength to be measured only by election results. Socialist newspapers were widely read. The *Appeal to Reason* alone had a circulation of more than 500,000 by 1912. However, by the time Debs and other local candidates had made the Socialist party a force almost comparable in strength to the Populists of the 1890s, a number of the more militant socialists had already left it for groups advocating violent revolution, while some of the more conservative members drifted into the Democratic ranks, attracted by Wilsonian reforms.

Haywood and others in the Western Federation of Miners had advocated bringing skilled and unskilled workers into a single fighting organization. In 1905, with Debs's backing, Haywood, Daniel De Leon and others formed the Industrial Workers of the World, a union dedicated to militant action for the overthrow of capitalism. Just as the I.W.W. was getting started, Haywood and two other men, Charles Moyer and George Pettibone, were arrested in Denver, spirited away illegally to Idaho, and put on trial for the dynamite murder of Frank Steunenberg, former governor of Idaho. Defended by the brilliant Chicago lawyer Clarence Darrow, the three men were eventually acquitted. But a number of more conservative socialists had split with the I.W.W. in a dispute over the goals of unionism. By the time Haywood resumed his activities, the organization was thoroughly dominated by extreme radicals. The Socialist party broke with the I.W.W. for good in 1908.

"Wobblies," as the I.W.W.'s members were called, found support in mills, mines and lumbering camps, especially in the West, where they advocated sabotage and uncompromising war against capitalism. In cities up and down the Pacific Coast they staged "free speech" demonstrations between 1909 and 1912. A few Wobblies would slip into town, make soapbox speeches and get themselves arrested. Then hundreds of others would flood the town and commit the same offense until the jails were overflowing and the local citizens were fighting among themselves about the best way to curb I.W.W. agitation.

Though the total number in the I.W.W. probably never exceeded 50,000, the organization made itself felt as few other groups have. A measure of the fear it inspired is the fact that between 1917 and 1920, no fewer than 18 states and two territories passed criminal syndicalism laws, making I.W.W. activity punishable with jail terms of up to 25 years.

Early in the century the *Appeal to Reason* had predicted the inevitability of a Socialist triumph. Measured by the vote for Debs in 1912, American socialism did in fact make great strides both in the city and the country. Nevertheless something was lacking. The Socialist party never seemed to have the potential to win national power as the Labourites were to do in England and the Social Democrats in Germany. The reasons are varied. Local leaders, though uniting behind Debs every four years, remained too divided between elections and too dogmatic to make the compromises necessary for continuing, effective political action on a national scale. Some historians have argued that the American dream was too powerful, and that the underprivileged, no matter how bad their plight, dreamed of a day when they might be capitalists themselves. Perhaps, in competition with other, less radical movements, socialism in America simply failed to attract enough intellectuals with strong leadership ability. In any case, after 1912 it was clear that socialism had failed to build a powerful national party of workers and farmers for political action against the rich.

THERE was another form of action open to the underprivileged. Owners of a railroad or factory or mine were dependent on the workers who made the machines run. If the workers united in demanding better conditions or higher wages, their employers would have to give in. So at least ran the arguments behind the efforts to organize a national labor union from the 1860s into the 1890s. At times this program of collective bargaining was coupled with others, including socialist projects. Probably the most idealistic concept had been embraced by the Knights of Labor, the union group that wanted workingmen to join forces with farmers, small businessmen and all other victims of big business (except "non-toilers" like lawyers and saloonkeepers). But gradually the notion of particular groups of workers negotiating with their employers took new form and emerged as a quest limited to higher wages, shorter hours and improved working conditions—the so-called "pure and simple unionism" of the American Federation of Labor.

Nationwide unions of carpenters, bricklayers, typographers, iron molders,

Defense attorney Clarence Darrow won acquittal for Haywood after an 80-day trial. Later Darrow was accused of tampering with the jury. Prosecutor Borah (below), recalling Darrow's angry arguments, denied the charge, saying, "Darrow didn't bribe these jurors, he frightened them to death."

William E. Borah, who prosecuted "Big Bill" Haywood unsuccessfully, was warned to protect himself against pro-union gunmen said to be seeking revenge. Borah sardonically retorted to Governor Gooding: "These people would not be interested in killing a prosecutor when a governor is available."

cigarmakers and other craftsmen joined together in the AFL. Most of these craft unions were tightly knit and, within limits, could make employers meet their terms or suffer a strike. Although the various craft unions had enrolled only a few hundred thousand members before 1900, their hope was that, through the AFL, they could unionize other trades. Through a strong labor movement, they expected to gain a general improvement in the economic and social status of skilled workers, and ultimately uplift all the impoverished. In reality, the AFL was more a pledge of allegiance to these goals than an instrument for attaining them. Its president Samuel Gompers, an English-born cigarmaker, dedicated his life to making the AFL an effective force for labor's advancement. But the constituent unions were jealous of their independence and reluctant to reduce their own strike funds in order to build up the treasury of the parent body. Gompers had to spend most of his time proving to the rank and file that a national organization was worthwhile.

Labor's power was actually in the hands of the individual unions. From 1900 to 1905 hardly a week passed without one craft or another demanding higher wages or shorter hours or a closed shop. Few cities failed to experience at least one serious strike; no one who read city newspapers could escape exposure to labor's claim to a fairer share in the nation's prosperity or capital's counterclaim that unions constituted monopolies in restraint of commerce and, at least potentially, menaces to the American way of life. Two strikes attracted special notice, and, though they involved larger stakes than most, they were fairly representative of the character of labor strife of the time.

Around the turn of the century, coal miners like the one above "were brought into the world by the company doctor, lived in a company house or hut, were nurtured by the company store . . . laid away in the company graveyard." In their revolt against this rule, the miners became the "shock troops of American labor," winning 160 of 260 disputes in 1898.

THE Amalgamated Association of Iron, Steel and Tin Workers counted as members most of the skilled rollers and puddlers. At one time it had been able to force favorable terms from almost all steelmakers. Then Andrew Carnegie's company took the lead in mechanizing steelmaking to decrease dependence on skilled hands. Little by little Carnegie drove the union out of his plants, and other companies, watching this union retreat, became better able to resist union demands. In 1901, when J. P. Morgan created United States Steel, it seemed as if the union might be broken altogether.

T. J. Shaffer, a onetime clergyman who headed the Amalgamated, decided that this was the time to fight. Since it was important for the newly formed U.S. Steel to be able to float securities, Shaffer calculated that Morgan and his associates might make concessions in order to prevent a strike. Testing this hypothesis, Shaffer demanded that the Amalgamated be recognized as a bargaining agent in all hoop, tin-plate and sheet-steel plants, union and nonunion alike, and that the company guarantee uniform wage scales.

The steel industry's management was anti-union on principle. But Shaffer was right in his guess that U.S. Steel wanted no interruption of production: the Executive Committee offered a compromise covering unionized plants. Shaffer, recognizing the realities of the situation, began to negotiate with individual mills. However, the head of one mill refused to compromise. Shaffer had no choice but to carry out his threat and call a strike in the sheet mills. Every member of the union walked out, and, surprisingly, many nonmembers joined them. All sheet mills and all but one hoop mill, union and nonunion, were shut down.

Now the financiers did step in. Overruling plant executives, they insisted on substantial compromise. The company offered to negotiate contracts for all union mills and some nonunion mills. Shaffer, confident that his strategy would succeed, reiterated his original demand for contracts covering all non-union mills. When the company said it could go no further, the union added a strike call for tin-plate workers, shutting down still more plants. This turned out to be a blunder. For, concluding that the union wanted too much, the financiers turned matters back to the plant managers. The managers brought in scabs and soon had the mills working again.

Then Shaffer met with Morgan and reached agreement on a compromise: The union would call off the strike in return for contracts at certain of the union mills. Outraged, other officers of the union repudiated the agreement on the ground that the company was offering less than the terms earlier rejected. Morgan believed that Shaffer had broken faith and closed his mind to further negotiations. The union, forced to capitulate on management's terms, was left in a shambles. Organized labor, it seemed, could not beat industry.

T HE second major strike, however, had a different outcome for several reasons. The United Mine Workers of America was a growing union; the steelworkers had been losing members. The steel union was restricted to skilled men; the miners welcomed to membership almost anyone who had anything to do with coal mining. Finally, the miners had behind them a record of recent successes in achieving higher pay scales in the soft-coal fields and the union's chief, John Mitchell, was ready to take on the hard-coal operators. Mostly railroad companies, they were fewer and stronger than the soft-coal owners. But anthracite miners were less united than those in soft-coal districts, for Catholic members traditionally fought with Protestants, native Americans with immigrants and immigrant groups with one another.

With a small group of picked men Mitchell visited every hard-coal town, talking about what a union could accomplish, signing up recruits. Between natives and immigrants he drew no distinction. "The coal you dig isn't Slavish or Polish or Irish coal," he insisted, "it's coal."

Mitchell had a way of listening to what everyone said, paying attention to men not used to attention and answering objections thoughtfully. His persuasive powers were formidable, and in public debate he converted many anti-union people to his side. In 1900 he presented modest demands to the anthracite operators. When these were disregarded, the union voted to strike. Over 100,000 union and nonunion men walked out, and the operators, though refusing to acknowledge the existence of the union, posted notices announcing pay scales similar to those Mitchell had asked. The strike was halted.

Early in 1902 Mitchell made new demands, this time for a 20 per cent pay increase, an eight-hour day and, above all, recognition of the union as the bargaining agent for its members. Although the owners refused to deal with him, he delayed his strike call until miners lost their patience and overrode his counsels of delay. When the call went out, the response was even better than in 1900. Some 150,000 miners left the pits, and obeying rules Mitchell laid down, they stayed home, made few demonstrations and did nothing to provoke violence from the guards and police the operators brought in. Mitchell's strategy was to put the blame on the operators and so get the public on his side. Inevitably, he believed, public opinion would force politicians and financiers to put pressure on the operators. Through every medium he circulated details about the sorry conditions under which miners

John Mitchell, who became president of the United Mine Workers of America in 1898, fought to end child labor in the mines. He himself had worked in an Illinois mine at the age of 12, a year before the state law permitted. Recalling this, he once said he "would rather be able to take the little boys out of the breakers than name the next President of the United States."

worked to prove that the miners were only appealing for simple justice.

Despite the rising tension, Mitchell never lost his composure. A thin man, always dressed in somber black, he was often mistaken by immigrants for a priest. His mental attitudes called to mind Lincoln. But underneath he was never really calm. When troubles mounted, insomnia plagued him. (A few years later he took to whisky as an opiate and died at 49.) While the strike went on, he closed his eyes only in exhaustion.

Mitchell faced a problem within his union. Many soft-coal miners wanted to declare a sympathy strike in support of the anthracite miners and stop all production. But the union had contracts with the soft-coal companies, and Mitchell felt a strike would destroy their repeated contention that unions could make bargains and keep them. A soft-coal strike or a wave of strikes would, he thought, harm people who had nothing to do with the anthracite industry and turn the public against the miners.

INSTRUCTING THE BROTHER.

FIRE IN THE HOLE BUDDY.

LOADING HIS TURN.

These idealized vignettes, from an early certificate of membership in the United Mine Workers of America, depict the union miner's work as being more gracious than grubby. Such visionary versions of life in the pits reflected the UMW's promise to its rank and file that through the union they would achieve far more than "a kick in the pants and a crust of bread."

SHORTLY after the anthracite strike began, soft-coal locals demanded a convention. Fearful that the outcome of such a meeting would be a vote for a sympathy strike, Mitchell delayed convening the delegates until the hard-coal strike was seven weeks old. Rising before the assembly, Mitchell made his appeal. What the strikers needed, he said, was money to enable them to hold out. The soft-coal miners could help most by staying at their jobs, earning all they could, and contributing either 10 per cent of their wages or a dollar a week. Union officers pledged themselves to donate 35 per cent of their salaries. His words told. Undecided delegations announced their opposition to a sympathy strike. The meeting ended with a resounding vote in favor of Mitchell's plan.

However it took time for the money to come in and the union's war chest melted away. Strikers went hungry, tempers frayed and occasionally violence erupted. Wagons carrying the household goods of strikebreakers onto mine property were overturned. Some scabs had their outhouses dynamited. Rotten tomatoes were hurled at company police and troopers. It became increasingly doubtful that the miners could hold out or that, if they did, their passions would stay in check.

Then the dollars began to pour in from the soft-coal fields. At Gompers' urging, other AFL unions helped. Ultimately, more than $2.5 million came in, and strikers' families again had food on their tables. Mitchell's reputation soared. Moreover, he was achieving his objective. Winter was approaching and people in cities shivered in anticipation of cold houses. Congressmen up for re-election, financiers and industrialists thinking about profits for the coming months—all were concerned. But thanks to Mitchell's tactics, public opinion remained favorable to the union.

The operators, on the other hand, had alienated almost everyone. They had blustered about anarchism and radicalism, of which most reporters and investigators could find little trace. George F. Baer, the president of the Reading Railway, which controlled half the hard-coal mines, had hurt the owners' cause irreparably by his reply to a citizen who urged concessions: "The rights and interests of the laboring man will be protected and cared for—not by the labor agitators, but by the Christian men to whom God in His infinite wisdom has given the control of the property interests of the country. . . ." The operators seemed to confuse themselves with the Almighty.

On October 3 President Theodore Roosevelt invited Mitchell and the leading operators to meet in Washington. The union leader declared that his men would accept whatever a government-appointed board of arbitration ruled, provided the operators agreed to do likewise. The operators huffed that they would not deal with "a set of outlaws," and the meeting adjourned without result. After the meeting was over, President Roosevelt said of George Baer's conduct: "If it wasn't for the high office I hold, I would have taken him by the seat of the breeches and the nape of the neck and chucked him out of [the] window." But other conferences soon followed, including one held on J. P. Morgan's yacht. In the end the operators caved in and agreed to accept federal arbitration.

Then the operators balked at putting a representative of labor on the board: Mitchell could not accept less. But the operators had originally consented to the appointment of an "eminent sociologist," and they did not renege when the man selected proved to be Edgar E. Clark, the head of the Order of Railway Conductors.

On October 23, 1902, the miners returned to their jobs after 23 weeks of struggle. Five months later the arbitrators rendered their verdict: a 10 per cent increase in pay, a nine-hour day for most, the right of miners to name checkweighmen to oversee the weighing of coal and a conciliation board to be formed for hearing workers' grievances.

This was less than Mitchell had demanded, though more than he had been ready to settle for. From his standpoint the only really bad feature was that the operators were not required to recognize the union, but he got around this by insisting that mine-union officers be the labor representatives on the conciliation board. There were other achievements of great significance: Reformers like Henry Demarest Lloyd and Clarence Darrow had come to the aid of the miners; an American President had taken a fair and impartial part in a labor dispute. These actions were a harbinger of the changing attitudes that would produce the progressive movement. On the whole, the outcome of the strike was a tremendous triumph not only for the miners and for trade unionism, but for the whole reform movement.

Hard-boiled George Baer, representing the mine owners, refused to talk with striking miners in 1902. This cartoon urges Baer to choose a cookie labeled "Arbitration" instead of the one he is reaching for —"Unconditional Surrender." Ultimately Baer had to negotiate, but not before he scoffed at the miners, saying: "They don't suffer; why, they can't even speak English."

UNFORTUNATELY it was a short-lived victory. Employers closed ranks. Forming trade associations, they exchanged information about union organizers, built up black lists, supplied one another with strikebreakers and formed common fronts against labor demands. More broadly based organizations such as the National Association of Manufacturers fed anti-union publicity to the press. In the Danbury Hatters and the Buck's Stove and Range cases, the courts outlawed boycotts and upheld the right of judges to enjoin strikes. Violence gave a bad odor to all labor activity, especially after 1911, when a member of an AFL union, James B. McNamara, confessed to having thrown a bomb the previous year into the Los Angeles *Times* building, killing 21 people. AFL membership, which had gone from less than 400,000 in the late '90s to more than 1.6 million in 1904, ceased to rise and even declined a bit in the years that followed. Organized labor's balance sheet up to the time of World War I was hardly encouraging reading. Although they could count more success than socialism, the unions had accomplished relatively little in the way of raising living standards for the millions who were poor. The "other half" would have to look elsewhere for help.

An anonymous radical of 1914 uses a primitive method to advertise a threatening slogan of the I.W.W.

Angry years of social turmoil

Socialism is coming . . . and nothing can stop it . . . you can feel it in the air . . . you can taste it in the price of beef. . . ." So wrote a prophet of the Left in 1902. Many Americans, alarmed by a few bomb-throwing anarchists, considered anyone who threatened the status quo a dangerous radical. Yet it was a time when some considered radicalism the only adequate response to the abuses of big business, which concentrated immense power and wealth in the hands of the few men who dominated the nation's economy. The results—which included appalling working conditions, child labor and brutal strikebreaking—seemed to be inherent in the capitalist system itself.

To the "Wobblies" of the I.W.W. (Industrial Workers of the World) it followed that it was "the historic mission of the working class to do away with capitalism." Although the Socialists broke with the I.W.W. over proper union aims, their political program called for the attainment of many I.W.W. goals through the ballot box. In 1912 the leftward wave reached its crest, as Socialist Eugene Debs polled nearly 6 per cent of the votes for President. Eventually, certain radical demands were adopted by the moderate unions and the major political parties. Many radicals, accepting reform rather than insisting on revolution, slowly drifted into the mainstream of the labor movement.

LABOR'S "JOAN OF ARC," Elizabeth Gurley Flynn, addresses striking textile workers in Lawrence, Massachusetts. The great victory in this 1912 strike heartened radicals.

A strikers' tent colony at Ludlow is shown before the company-paid militia attacked it on April 20, 1914. Here some 1,200 workers of 21

The ruins of Ludlow are seen after the slaughter ended. During the 14-hour attack cellars and trenches gave some cover, but women and

nationalities were knit together by hunger and a common cause.

children "died like trapped rats when the flames swept over them."

Merciless strikebreaking in Colorado mine towns

THE threat of radicalism provided some industrialists with an excuse for ruthlessly suppressing labor's demands for humane reform. In September 1913, for example, some 9,000 miners in the coal fields of southern Colorado went on strike to improve their working conditions and to win company recognition of their union, the United Mine Workers. Anticipating eviction from company-owned houses, the miners moved into crude tent colonies built near the company towns. The mine operators promptly recruited armed guards.

The main encampment at Ludlow *(left)*, near the Colorado Fuel and Iron Company, was sporadically harassed for seven months. While the strikers were still hoping for a settlement, on April 20, 1914, they were suddenly attacked by 200 company guards. This private army raked the tents with gunfire for hours, then soaked them with kerosene and set them ablaze. When the shooting finally stopped, at least 21 were dead and 100 wounded. Although the strike continued for nearly eight months, the operators eventually won.

RETRIEVING A MINER'S BODY, a striker waves a truce flag at Forbes, Colorado, in October 1913. The miner was killed by bullets from the "Death Special," the company's armored car.

Anarchist Alexander Berkman addresses a crowd in New York. Berkman, who had been jailed for attempted murder, was later deported.

CHILD SYMPATHIZERS wear banners during a 1916 strike *(left)* condemning anti-union scab activity. "A scab in labor unions," said Debs, "means the same as a traitor to his country."

Protests, parades and a handful of dynamite

ALL labor factions used the strike, and almost all the boycott, as their most effective instruments of combat. But there were other forms of protest too. Samuel Gompers, leader of the AFL, told Socialists, "Economically you are unsound, socially you are wrong, industrially you are an impossibility." He encouraged the techniques of moderation: lobbying, negotiation, pamphleteering and, somewhat melodramatically, the occasional recruitment of children as strike sympathizers *(below, left)*. But the activities of the radicals spanned a broader spectrum of revolt. They included annual parades *(below)*, appeals to exploited immigrants in their native tongues *(opposite)* and an occasional extremist act of terrorism like the bombing shown at right.

TERRORIST AND VICTIM—an innocent bystander—lie dead on a New York street. The picture was taken seconds after the would-be assassin's bomb exploded in his hand at a rally.

SOCIALIST GIRLS march in a New York May Day parade early in the 20th Century. In 1886 workers in the U.S. turned out on May Day to demand the eight-hour day. As a result the Socialist International congress chose May 1 as a world labor holiday in 1889. From 1890 on, aided by a vigorous campaign by Samuel Gompers, such demonstrations became widespread.

ON THE PLATFORM, Gene Debs (*above*) makes an impassioned appeal to his audience. According to reporter Lincoln Steffens, Debs's power as an orator lay in "the feeling he conveys that he feels for his fellow men; as he does, desperately."

ON TOUR, Debs (*opposite*) delivers a campaign speech at Momence, Illinois, in 1908. Despite its all-out efforts in this election, the Socialist party barely increased its 1904 vote. But in 1912, it would more than double the total vote of 1908.

THE "RED SPECIAL," used by Debs in his 1908 campaign, is surrounded by followers (*left*). To discredit Debs, who had traveled a grueling 9,000 miles in less than four weeks, a Detroit newspaper criticized his use of a "magnificent palace car."

Debs: apostle of peace and socialist crusader

TALL, lean and supple, Eugene V. Debs was a giant among labor leaders and radical politicians for more than four decades. At the age of 19, after three years as a locomotive fireman, he helped organize a local of the Fireman's Brotherhood and soon became its national secretary. In 1892 he formally broke with trade unionism—"the aristocrats of labor"—and in 1893 set up the industry-wide American Railway Union. While in jail for defying a court injunction during the Pullman strike of 1894, he turned toward socialism. He joined in founding the socialistic Industrial Workers of the World and the Socialist party. He was Socialist candidate for President in five elections—the last time while serving a sentence in Atlanta Penitentiary (*right*) for speaking against World War I and the government's prosecution of dissenters. Theodore Roosevelt considered him simply an "undesirable citizen." But to followers he was the "living link between God and man."

IN PRISON, presidential candidate Debs embraces visitor Seymour Stedman, who was his running mate in 1920. Debs was released the following year.

At Lawrence, triumph, and then a slow decline

THE high-water mark of the radical labor movement was reached in the mill town of Lawrence, Massachusetts, in 1912. On January 12, thousands of workers —men, women and children—left their looms to protest a reduction in wages. In the next few weeks a group of top I.W.W. organizers arrived—among them Bill Haywood, Elizabeth Gurley Flynn, Joe Ettor and Arturo Giovannitti. Alarmed, the mayor called for additional state militia *(right)*. Ettor, omitting the usual I.W.W. warning that it would meet violence with violence, urged the workers to "make this strike as peaceful as possible." After management attempted to reopen the mills, police and strikers clashed and one woman was killed.

By March 12, nationwide sympathy for the strikers forced the mill owners to grant them wage increases of up to 25 per cent. But the triumph was brief. Wartime harassment almost destroyed the I.W.W. while boom times and patriotism combined to ease labor tensions.

PITTSBURGH STREETCAR WORKERS appeal for support during a walkout to secure increased wages in 1919. The brief strike failed—among other reasons, for lack of public support.

STRIKERS WITH FLAGS confront the Massachusetts militia at Lawrence. The workers heeded their leaders' warnings against starting violence and won public support.

3. PROGRESSIVISM AT THE GRASS ROOTS

ETWEEN the very few who possessed immense wealth and the teeming masses of working poor stood the large and varied groups that made up the middle classes—farm owners, storekeepers, clergymen, lawyers, doctors, teachers, salesmen and others. At the beginning of the 20th Century, almost all of these solid and industrious people were enjoying nearly unprecedented prosperity. Nevertheless, there were many in their ranks who were unhappy about what was happening in America.

The middle classes had been repelled by the Populist agitation of the '90s. When William Jennings Bryan became the Democratic nominee in 1896, his platform took over some Populist planks, including not only protests against abuses practiced by railroads and big corporations but also proposals for inflating the currency to help debtors against creditors. Interpreting this program as revolutionary, the urban middle classes voted McKinley into office. This result, coupled with Democratic defeats in state and local elections, seemed to show that the people of farm areas would not be able to carry through a program of reform unaided. But reform was in the air, and in a curious way the setbacks suffered by the Populists and Bryan Democrats paved the way for a broader movement. The "radicals" were discredited. The cause of reform could thus be taken up by respectable citizens. Looking back later, William Allen White, the Emporia, Kansas, newspaperman, would be able to remark that discontent had "shaved its whisk-

A HARDY HOMESTEADER in this detail of Harvey Dunn's
Old Settlers suggests the strength of the progressive movement that swept the United States in the early 1900s.

ers, washed its shirt, put on a derby and moved up into the middle class."

For reasons that can only be guessed, many middle-class Americans broke with conservative ways of thinking. They suddenly responded to the appeals of reformers. It may be that they were prompted, consciously or unconsciously, by resentment at the fact that their traditional prestige and status were being undermined by the steady increase in the power of the very rich. It may be, too, that the middle classes felt threatened by those at the other end of the economic spectrum, traditionally considered inferior, who were making ominous political, financial and social encroachments in areas from which they had formerly been barred.

With the exception of those who arrived with a skilled trade, mid-19th Century immigrants from Ireland, Germany and Scandinavia had done the dirty jobs in cities and mines and formed a pool from which well-off families of older stock recruited their gardeners, stable hands, coachmen and household servants. Now, however, the children of these immigrants were coming up in the world, becoming educated, acquiring property and moving into neighborhoods, schools, jobs, even private clubs that had once been Anglo-Saxon preserves. In Boston the Irish became so powerful politically that in 1905 they elected as mayor John F. "Honey Fitz" Fitzgerald; his grandson, John Fitzgerald Kennedy, would one day become the first Catholic President. In New York City Irish leadership of Tammany Hall, begun by Boss Tweed in 1863, was extended by John Kelly, Richard Croker and Charles Murphy well into the 20th Century. To a greater or lesser extent the same thing happened in Philadelphia, Chicago and other cities.

IN these places indignant citizens, led by descendants of the old families, had fought a losing battle. At first they campaigned against native-born politicians who, while helping the immigrants, exploited their ignorance and poverty and marshaled them into voting blocs supporting corrupt machines. Occasionally the campaigns for good government succeeded. Seldom, however, was the effect lasting. In a term or two the rascals were back, usually in greater strength than before, and as the machines came more and more to be manned and controlled by immigrant groups, reform campaigns took on an anti-foreign and anti-Catholic coloration. While suspicion and intolerance of immigrant groups never disappeared completely from reform groups it was soon apparent that bigotry was not the road to reform. The progressive movement offered far greater possibilities for a nationwide attack on the political power of the plutocracy—a power that sometimes extended to the financing and support of corrupt political machines.

Others also were drawn to progressivism. In time the movement was to encompass prohibitionists, advocates of women's rights, businessmen angry over competition from the trusts, professional politicians who saw in it a means of gaining votes and many others, not least among whom were men and women moved by nothing but compassion for the sweatshop worker and the child in the mill. Progressivism united many different impulses, but in broad terms it was a movement to remake America in a homogeneous, classless and virtuous image.

Progressive movements developed in a number of states at roughly the same time. Mayor Hazen Pingree of Detroit attacked public utility companies in the early 1890s. During the Panic of 1893, he instituted work-relief

A fanatical prohibitionist, Carry A. Nation grimly grips her favorite weapon of reform, a hatchet. Besides wrecking saloons, she issued bitter attacks on tobacco and lust. She called Daniel Webster a drunkard and Theodore Roosevelt a divekeeper, and she claimed that McKinley would have survived his assassin's bullet except that "his blood was bad from nicotine."

for the poor. Later, as governor of Michigan, he spent two terms unsuccessfully battling big business. By the turn of the century, Governor Theodore Roosevelt of New York sponsored laws to impose taxes on the franchises of public utility corporations and to improve conditions in urban tenements. But neither Pingree nor Roosevelt was considered the prophet of a new cause. Robert M. La Follette of Wisconsin was.

A SMALL wiry man with a big head made even bigger by a bush of hair, La Follette had started as a moderately successful Republican politician. After serving as a district attorney, he spent three terms in Congress before he was defeated in 1890 in a Democratic sweep of the state. Returned to private life, he harbored ambitions to return to the House or perhaps even to become governor or United States senator.

Then, in 1891, an event occurred which changed La Follette's whole life. Senator Philetus Sawyer, a millionaire lumberman who was a boss of the state Republican party, offered the 36-year-old lawyer a fee. At the time, Sawyer had an interest in a case to which La Follette's brother-in-law had been assigned as a judge. Though Sawyer denied the charge, La Follette interpreted the offer as a bribe and vehemently rejected it. He then reported the incident both to his brother-in-law and to the newspapers.

Sawyer, furious, tried to kill La Follette's political career. But La Follette was a hard man to down. Working tirelessly, he built up an organization of his own in farm districts as well as in Madison, Milwaukee and many Wisconsin towns. By 1900 he entered the Republican state convention with a majority of delegates pledged to his nomination for the governorship. Bowing to the inevitable, the regulars came to his support, and in November he was elected by a plurality of 102,000 votes.

Already calling himself a progressive, La Follette entered office determined to give the public greater control over the government. Under the prevailing system, candidates for public office were all too often chosen by convention delegates representing only bosses or at best party workers. La Follette advocated direct primaries—elections in which nominees would be selected by the voters. In time he would also advocate the initiative, which would permit citizens to propose their own bills, and the referendum, which would allow the entire electorate to register its opinion by balloting on measures already passed by the legislature.

Above all, La Follette wanted government to become the public's shield against powerful economic interests. He believed that government could work effectively to restore healthy competition where big business had destroyed it. For certain large industries where monopolistic power was inevitable—especially the railroads—he wanted strong government regulations enacted to compel maximum service at minimum cost.

In his first term as governor, La Follette did not press for his whole program. A practical politician, he recognized the wisdom of waging one battle at a time. He also knew that certain items on his agenda would meet defeat in the upper house. So he concentrated on the two measures that enjoyed the most widespread popular support—the proposal for a direct primary and a bill requiring railroad companies to pay taxes based on the physical values of their properties rather than, as in the past, on their gross earnings.

Both issues provoked determined opposition, especially in the Wisconsin

Susan B. Anthony, furnished with Uncle Sam's hat in this cartoon, devoted 70 years to crusading for reform. Her chief campaigns were for abolition, temperance, religious tolerance and above all equal rights for women. Only four states had given women the vote by 1900, but Miss Anthony's efforts had won wide respect and affection, even from those opposed to her.

Promising reform, Tom L. Johnson was elected mayor of Cleveland in 1901. Promptly he summoned the city's saloonkeepers and offered a bargain: If they promised to keep order, to prohibit gambling machines and pay no blackmail to his own police, he would ignore minor legal infractions. Johnson's shrewd realism helped him give Cleveland a model city government.

senate. Old Guard Republicans and Democrats joined to fight them. Railroad officials, foreseeing the increased taxes their companies would have to pay, put all their resources behind an intensive and successful lobbying drive. Both measures were killed, and no important progressive legislation was passed. Running for re-election in 1902, La Follette attacked the forces arrayed against him and asked the voters to back him up with a legislature committed to his program.

His vigorous campaign was effective in reducing the number of opponents in the new assembly and senate. During his second term La Follette once again demanded direct primary and railroad tax legislation. In a strong message he also asked for creation of a commission to regulate railroad rates and standards of service. Despite the election results, it took hard fighting to get the direct primary law on the books. The railroad taxation act went through only after the companies gave in on that issue in order to concentrate on fighting regulation. This they were able to defeat.

La Follette had made some progress, and, as the campaign of 1904 approached, he worked to elect a legislature that would enact the rest of his program. Since the primary law was not yet in effect, nominees would still be chosen by a party convention. Up and down the state La Follette appealed for the election of men he could work with. His method was to take the platform and recite for the audience the voting record of the legislators he opposed, concluding, "Put the men who have betrayed you on the retired list."

Republican party regulars, supported by the railroads, launched a counterattack. At the state convention they tried desperately to prevent La Follette's renomination. Failing in that, they tried to put a second Republican candidate into the race. When the state supreme court ruled La Follette the legal candidate, most of the regulars deserted party ranks and supported the Democratic candidate. La Follette won by a narrower margin than in either of the previous elections. But he did win, took into office with him a sympathetic house and senate, and was able to push through one bill after another. By the time La Follette moved on to the United States Senate in 1906, Wisconsin had added to its list of reform laws one measure establishing a strong railroad commission, another law requiring lobbyists to register and a third requiring competitive examinations for the state civil service.

THE example set by La Follette for the nation was just as important as the specific measures he enacted. He proved that a reform movement could win elections (the La Follette organization would dominate Wisconsin for more than two decades) and that good legislation could not only be passed but honestly enforced by dedicated men. He also demonstrated that government could be an independent force capable of coping on behalf of the average citizen with ruthless business combines.

People across the country talked about "the Wisconsin Idea"—the belief that government could, as La Follette wrote, see to it that a state becomes "a happier and better state to live in, that its institutions are more democratic, that the opportunities of all its people are more equal, that social justice more nearly prevails, that human life is safer and sweeter. . . ."

Working along similar lines at city levels were other progressives. Toledo had Samuel M. Jones, a big, fair-haired Welshman who placarded his factory with the injunction, "Therefore, whatsoever things ye would that men should do unto you, do ye even so to them." Jones carried out this precept by paying maximum wages, maintaining an eight-hour day, giving vacations with pay, providing recreational facilities for workmen and their families, instituting profit sharing among them and eliminating timekeepers. When elected mayor in 1897, he applied the golden rule to the city. He conducted drives for better schools, parks and recreation facilities. To encourage more humane treatment of lawbreakers, he took away policemen's nightsticks. When he sat as a magistrate, he preferred to lecture offenders and then release them. More alarmingly, from the standpoint of those who had put him in office, he refused to sanction the customary deals for patronage, public works contracts and utility franchises. He advocated a municipal civil service, insisted on open bidding for public works and freely asserted his belief that all utilities should be publicly owned.

Although his party's leaders refused to renominate him in 1899, he ran as an independent, beat all his opponents and repeated this feat in three consecutive elections. Even his death in office in 1904 did not break his hold, for the voters chose one of his lieutenants and disciples, Brand Whitlock, to take his place.

GOLDEN RULE " JONES'S eccentricities made him an unlikely model for reformers in other cities and towns. But a man who could not be considered a crank came forward in Cleveland, the headquarters from which Mark Hanna, the national Republican party boss, ran his Ohio organization. This hardheaded idealist was industrialist Tom L. Johnson.

The son of a Kentucky slaveowner ruined by the Civil War, Johnson had had to start work as a boy without the advantage of much formal education. But he learned to be a good mechanic and, more important, a capable bookkeeper. As a youngster working for the Louisville Street Railway Company, he invented a fare box with glass traps for use on trolleys and buses. The invention made him a capitalist. By shrewd investment, he gradually acquired street railways in Brooklyn, Cleveland, Indianapolis and Detroit. He was a big man in this booming field, and he earned a reputation as a smart and ruthless operator.

In Cleveland Johnson's fight with Hanna had ended with Johnson controlling most of the city's lines. Both men used the word "consolidated" in their company titles, and Johnson's was known as the Big Con, Hanna's as the Little Con. Later Johnson sold out, the two companies merged and the new firm was called the Concon.

Then, on a train trip, Johnson was persuaded to buy a copy of Henry George's *Social Problems* from a newsboy. After reading this and other explanations of George's theory that a single tax on land was the only way to break the power of unjust wealth, he became an enthusiastic convert and helped finance George's unsuccessful mayoralty campaign in New York. In 1890 Johnson himself got elected as a Democratic congressman so that he could espouse the single tax from a national forum. During most of this time politics was a hobby, and the business of making money in railways and steel remained his occupation. He served two terms in the House, then sold his various interests in order to devote full time to public service.

In 1901 he ran for mayor of Cleveland as a Democrat. Hanna warned his friends that Johnson would prove dangerous, but few businessmen took

Robert M. La Follette Sr., seen with Bob Jr. in 1904, raised both his sons amid constant politicking. When Bob Jr. became a candidate to complete his late father's Senate term, he was belittled as a youthful novice. To this criticism a family friend retorted: "Bob Jr. and Phil have had more experience in politics than any boys since the days of the Roman Senators."

Ida Tarbell, author of the devastating "History of the Standard Oil Company," had strong personal reasons for exposing the trust: Her father had been squeezed out of business by the oil interests. Yet she wrote her "History" without bias, insuring its place among the greatest works of its kind.

Ray Stannard Baker was a young reporter in Chicago when he began to "lift a flap of the gorgeous tent . . . and look into the cold, wet streets." Paid by the line, he drew $40 in one week while covering a restaurant strike. This immediately earned him a promotion to a staff job—for just $12 a week.

fright. It was hard for them to be suspicious of someone with so much money, and Johnson won easily. In office, however, he behaved exactly as Hanna had prophesied. Johnson shook out the time-servers and filled their places with energetic, determined and idealistic men. A clergyman became chief of prisons and charities, a shrewd young lawyer became city solicitor and a former professor of economics was brought in from New York to help with tax assessments. In short order the city's services were being performed more efficiently and petty corruption was practically at an end. An experienced journalist who visited Cleveland pronounced it the best-governed city in America.

JOHNSON'S ambitions went much further than merely providing better administration. Speaking from his own experience with franchise-holding utility companies, he declared: "I believe in municipal ownership of all public service monopolies for the same reason that I believe in the municipal ownership of waterworks, of parks, of schools. I believe in the municipal ownership of these monopolies because if you do not own them they will in time own you. They will rule your politics, corrupt your institutions and finally destroy your liberties."

Tom Johnson worked toward his objective by stages, beginning, as had La Follette, by demanding that the properties of public service corporations be fairly and objectively assessed for taxation. At hearing after hearing he attacked existing valuations, often with deadly effect. For example, after the Cleveland Belt and Terminal Railroad claimed that it was properly and accurately assessed at $19,655, Johnson proposed a much higher figure. Turning suavely to Myron T. Herrick, the company's board chairman, he said, "You will remember, Myron, how you and I tried to buy it about five years ago for five hundred thousand dollars, and we thought that was dirt cheap." Although state boards and courts prevented Cleveland from changing any assessments, the public revelations of business practices convinced many citizens that corporations enjoyed unfair privileges.

In this way Johnson laid the groundwork for his major campaigns for municipal ownership of electric power and street railways. A bond issue was proposed to the city council to provide funds for a public power plant. But the local electric light company managed to defeat the bond issue. When the Johnson forces decided to submit the issue to a referendum, the company got an injunction to stop the election. The injunction, moreover, was sustained by the state courts. Johnson then executed a flanking maneuver by annexing some adjoining villages that owned their own power plants, and despite ferocious attempts by the utility company to block this action, he was able to put his plan into operation.

In his dealings with his old comrades and rivals of the Concon street railway, Johnson was even more adroit. He granted a franchise to a new company which would guarantee a three-cent fare, two cents below the Concon's. It was his hope that stern new competition would weaken the older company, and that in the end the city would be able to lease both lines from their stockholders.

No quarter was asked or granted in the battle that followed. On one occasion a crew of the low-fare company was authorized to tear up a stretch of its rival's tracks. After years of struggle Johnson won, and the assets of both companies were surrendered to the Municipal Traction Company. And even then, Johnson's triumph was brief. Former directors of the Concon harassed the successor company. Clevelanders, expecting miraculous improvements, were disappointed. As Johnson observed sadly, people blamed him for every schedule delay. One man, he was told, fell off a car and exclaimed, "Damn Tom Johnson." Finally, in 1908, the people of Cleveland voted to return the streetcar system to private ownership, and a year later Johnson himself was defeated for re-election.

When Johnson's public career ended in 1909, the single tax was already a fading nostrum. Municipal ownership of utilities had not been helped by Cleveland's example, for private traction interests elsewhere used it as an argument in their favor. But Johnson, like La Follette, had inspired men all over the country to believe that government could help the public to protect itself against the economic aristocracy. Other reformers had organized vigorous campaigns like Johnson's in Boston, Springfield, New York, Jersey City, Philadelphia, Cincinnati, Kansas City, Milwaukee, Minneapolis, Denver and San Francisco.

Muckraker Lincoln Steffens was known as an outspoken man with a lively sense of humor. One day magnate Charles Mellen, whose railroads were plagued by rear-end collisions, sarcastically asked the reporter what he would do about the problem. "That's easy," said Steffens. "I'd cut off the last car."

OFTEN the progressives grew strong enough to dominate whole states. Albert B. Cummins captured the Republican party in Iowa, as did Hiram Johnson in California. In Kansas a group of vigorous young men led by newspaper publisher William Allen White scored similar victories. In Minnesota, North Dakota and Missouri, Democratic reform governors came into office. Elsewhere in the nation, even though they failed to win the governorship, reformers succeeded in forcing through their state legislatures such measures as the direct primary, initiative and referendum laws, tax reforms, and provisions for various regulatory commissions.

The programs of these reformers closely resembled La Follette's—more efficient government with broader representation to protect the public against the power of vested economic interests. The short space of time between La Follette's first term as governor and Johnson's last term as mayor had seen progressivism grow from a purely local manifestation to a significant national movement. Progressivism was a highly newsworthy topic, and enterprising publishers, ever on the lookout for circulation-building stories, scented a profitable field for investigation.

The development of mass circulation daily newspapers had brought in its train a keen competition for sensational exposés to titillate the public appetite and stimulate sales. When William Randolph Hearst and Joseph Pulitzer were battling for pre-eminence in New York City, they made a fine art of building circulation by exploiting sensation.

Reporter Burton J. Hendrick was often praised for his originality in showing the human side of unpopular "robber barons." But Hendrick was not trying to be original; he frankly admired his subjects. Eventually he deserted the ranks of muckrakers to become a sympathetic chronicler of big business.

Any sensation, any scandal, no matter how unconscionable, served Hearst's purposes. Yet he had a constructive side. His San Francisco *Examiner* was an untiring critic of the Southern Pacific Railroad, fighting its poor service and artificially high rates and its systematic corruption of state and local officials. In New York City Hearst's *Journal* battled the depredations of public utilities combines. From coast to coast, Hearst papers distinguished themselves in the early years of the century by combating monopolies, presenting the worker's side of labor-management disputes and espousing political, economic and social reforms.

For a time, Hearst himself seemed to be a prime candidate for leadership of a national left-wing movement, uniting the poor with some segments of the

These cartoons from "An Alphabet of Joyous Trusts" denounced the beef and drug combines. The cartoonist Frederick Opper added in verse: "With these alphabet pictures the artist took pains, / But he's got to stop now, and with grief nearly busts— / 'Cause our language but twenty-six letters contains, / Though our country contains twenty-six hundred Trusts."

middle class. He had none of the personal magnetism for such a calling, but through his papers he was becoming a voice of the people. Above all, he decided in his own mind that he ought to be a leader, and he set his sights on becoming President of the United States. He won two terms in Congress as a Democrat, but he failed in his try for the presidential nomination in 1904, and two successive defeats in campaigns for New York City's mayoralty and the state's governorship killed his presidential chances. By 1908 he was so estranged from the Democrats that he backed his own minuscule third party, the Independence League. From that time onward he was politically an Ishmael, whose hand was against every man. Perhaps because of the poison of frustration, he turned his papers toward sheer sensationalism and even attacked some of the causes he had once sponsored.

ALTHOUGH Hearst appalled progressives with his sordid sensationalism that built circulation, he deserves some credit for inspiring the vast exposé literature that marked the progressive era. But journalism's most significant contribution to the progressive cause came through the exposé articles published by monthly magazines from 1902 on and circulated to a nationwide audience of the literate public.

By 1906 Theodore Roosevelt was able to speak of certain writers of political exposés who reminded him of Bunyan's Man with the Muck-rake who, when offered a celestial crown, "would neither look up nor regard the crown he was offered, but continued to rake to himself the filth of the floor." T.R.'s label—"muckraker"—stuck. It was cherished, indeed, as a title of honor.

Muckraking flourished largely because the growth of the progressive movement had developed a market for it. Publishers of monthly magazines like *Munsey's*, *Cosmopolitan* and *McClure's* had learned in the '90s that they could reach a mass audience by cutting the cost of their publications and by broadening and simplifying contents. Constantly experimenting with means of reaching still larger numbers, magazines added tales of adventure by such writers as Rudyard Kipling and Robert Louis Stevenson, reproductions of famous paintings and finally exposés.

S.S. McClure was the one who discovered this last device. Although his own gifts were those of a promoter, he had an eye for talent. He realized that good articles could best be written by men combining the skills of reporter, researcher and short-story writer, and when he found such people, he hired them as full-time staff writers. On his staff, among others, was Ida M. Tarbell, a quiet woman who had been trained in historical research at the Sorbonne and had written a serious biography. Another staff writer was Lincoln Steffens, the California-born, European-educated former city editor of the New York *Commercial Advertiser*. Presumably he had been hired to be managing editor of *McClure's*, but McClure soon told him, "You may have been an editor. You may be an editor. But you don't know how to edit a magazine. . . . Get out of here, travel, go—somewhere. . . . Buy a railroad ticket, get on a train, and there, where it lands you, there you will learn to edit a magazine." These were wise words, since Steffens, while a competent editor, was a truly great reporter.

Because trusts were in the news, McClure assigned Ida Tarbell to work up a series on the Standard Oil Company. Though he knew that she was the daughter of an oil pioneer who had been victimized by the oil interests, Mc-

Clure did not expect her to write an attack; he simply guessed that quite a few people would be interested in the history of this trust.

Miss Tarbell approached the task as a scholar, searching out old court records, reports of legislative hearings and newspaper files. She conducted interviews, talking with enemies of the company, others who had been in it and left, and at length with Henry H. Rogers and also with others who ran Standard Oil. Finally she wrote up her findings in a detached manner. She set forth the record, the accusations that had been made and the explanations that company officials offered. The end product of her years of work was a damning indictment, for it left no doubt that Rockefeller's corporations had corrupted governments, extorted privileges and crushed competition.

Steffens had meanwhile roamed as far as Missouri and there stumbled on a story. Joseph W. Folk, a young prosecuting attorney in St. Louis, had just discovered and proved before juries that certain aldermen had taken bribes and, moreover, that the bribes had been proffered by rich, respected citizens. Steffens collaborated with a St. Louis reporter in writing up the story, and *McClure's* published it just one month before Ida Tarbell's first installment was to appear.

Readers did like it. So did McClure. Steffens was sent to do a sequel on Minneapolis, where reformers had succeeded in routing a mayor and police chief who had connived with criminals. The January 1903 issue of the magazine contained this article, the second installment of Miss Tarbell's Standard Oil study, and a piece by Ray Stannard Baker attacking the methods used by the mineworkers' union in the 1902 hard-coal strike. McClure inserted a brief editorial, remarking that it was coincidence that had brought the three pieces together, but pointing out how similar they were. They showed, he said, "Capitalists, workingmen, politicians, citizens—all breaking the law, or letting it be broken."

When sales of *McClure's* soared, other 10-cent monthlies copied its example. Almost no trust, no political machine was spared, and one sensation followed another. Chapters from *Frenzied Finance* by Thomas Lawson, a disillusioned stock manipulator, were serialized in *Everybody's*. In the same journal Charles Edward Russell wrote about the meat-packing monopoly, "The Greatest Trust in the World." Burton J. Hendrick in *McClure's* exposed the "Tontine," a system by which life insurance companies unscrupulously accumulated huge surpluses and used these assets for speculation in the stock market. *Collier's* and the *Ladies' Home Journal* ran articles on the rich patent medicine industry, "the poison trust," revealing how the companies misrepresented their products and used advertising pressure to prevent any unfavorable criticism by newspapers of their quack remedies. For *Cosmopolitan*, David Graham Phillips wrote a series of articles, published under the title *The Treason of the Senate*, in which he indicted leaders in the upper house of Congress as willing tools of great economic interests.

F OR a few years the hubbub raised by the muckrakers was intense. Millions learned about the methods of big business and the corrupt ties linking corporations and politicians. The progressive movement, already strong in city halls and state capitals, now was in a position to summon to political action on a national scale the great body of middle-class Americans whose consciences and fears had been aroused.

This 1905 cartoon, one of a series illustrating a "Collier's" exposé of patent medicines, pointed out the perils of using cheap alcohol and laudanum, an opium solution. The exposé quoted a coroner's report on a child in Cincinnati who "came to her death from the poisonous effects of opium, the result of drinking the contents of a bottle of Doctor Bull's Cough Syrup."

A RAPT AUDIENCE at a nickelodeon relishes a boisterous Keystone Comedy. The earliest five-cent theater opened in 1905 in Pittsburgh. That same year 300-odd nickelodeons opened in New York alone; attendance soared into the hundreds of thousands.

A heyday for mass entertainment

I HAVE constructed a little instrument," Thomas Edison wrote in 1893, "which I call a Kinetoscope, with a nickel and slot attachment. Some 25 have been made, but [I] am very doubtful if there is any commercial feature in it." That year the "little instrument," forerunner of the projector, presented the first film, accompanied with a primitive sound arrangement on a record. It featured a man sneezing. The movies altered the world of entertainment. Within a few years they were bringing slapstick comedy, Broadway plays, imperiled Pauline and Biblical spectaculars to millions of people who had never before been able to afford such fun. Movies became everyman's theater. By 1910, ten thousand American movie houses had weekly audiences of 10 million people. Like films, the phonograph also brought stars and classics to the masses. In 1906 Edison was apologizing for being two and a half million records behind in filling orders. Other, longer-established forms of entertainment—vaudeville, the circus and the stage—enjoyed boom years. Circuses, touring the nation in caravans of as many as 90 railroad cars, opened their shows with magnificent pageants. Barnum & Bailey's "Cleopatra" had a cast of over a thousand. "Great successes," said one impresario of the time, "are those that take hold of the masses, not the classes." At the start of the 20th Century, entertainment aimed at the masses took hold and flourished.

A TRIPLE-DECKER POSTER heralds the Big Show's arrival in town in 1907, the year Ringling bought out Barnum & Bailey. Circuses never surpassed their 1910 popularity.

A cluster of stars that brightened the stage

Ed Wynn, vaudeville buffoon, appears in a misfit suit as "The Perfect Fool."

IN the opening years of the 20th Century, vaudeville had a speed, charm, glitter and glare that it had not known before. Plain folks could get six acts of variety for a nickel; fancier fare cost up to a dollar. New York shipped both plain and fancy to the country's 2,000 theaters: talking dogs, acrobats, hoofers, singers, comedy teams and dramatic skits. Hammerstein's famous variety house, the Victoria, booked freaks, a fake Hindu, a man with a 17-foot beard and even "America's Worst Act," which had to be put on behind a net to catch the flying vegetables. The Victoria also boasted such stars as Weber and Fields, Buster Keaton, Charlie Chaplin and Houdini. Another "star factory" was Charles Frohman's Empire Theater. It became the home of dull plays lit with glittering names: Maude Adams, Ethel Barrymore, Otis Skinner, Richard Mansfield, among others. George M. Cohan's swift succession of brash musical comedies sounded a new, uniquely American note. The fierce competition for star billing was intensified by an influx of Europeans looking for fame and the big money.

The Florodora Sextette sets out to conquer New York City in 1900. Brought over from London, all six made wealthy marriages and retired.

MAUDE ADAMS plays the title role in James Barrie's *Peter Pan*. The play made her so famous from 1905 on that it was said "her popularity . . . amounts almost to . . . worship."

THE CASTLES, Vernon and Irene, introduce a new step. The most noted dancers of their era, they invented steps to go with ragtime music and helped make dancing fashionable.

George M. Cohan displays his electric stage presence. Born on July 4, he claimed the holiday as his own in his song, "Yankee Doodle Boy."

Age of the nickelodeon and the early film

MOVIE MANNERS are flashed on a slide while reels are being changed to teach nickelodeon etiquette. In movie "singalongs," slides also illustrated the lyrics of songs.

I N 1893, at a cost of less than $700, Thomas Edison built the world's first film studio. It stood in West Orange, New Jersey, and was a flimsy affair that could be rotated to follow the sun and so make use of its light for the photographic process. There Edison made films that recorded sneezes, kisses, dances, even a baby being bathed. By 1896 brief films were being shown as special "acts" in vaudeville. Audiences were astounded by the "living pictures."

Then, in the early 1900s, came a new advance in the industry. It was the photoplay, a silent film that through action and printed titles told a tale. *The Great Train Robbery* was the first of these; a success, it was quickly followed by a pack of Westerns, usually filmed around New York City. In 1913 a photoplay, *Quo Vadis?*, longer

Baby carriages wait in front of a city nickelodeon and boys wonder if "A Flirty Affliction" is for them. By 1907 nickelodeons drew a daily

than any that Americans had previously seen, arrived from Italy. The high point of this epic was a thrilling chariot race. To meet this competition, America began producing its own spectaculars. Of these, D. W. Griffith's 1915 production *The Birth of a Nation* was the boldest, the most controversial and the most successful. It remains a classic. Comedies, produced casually, spontaneously, rapidly, emerged like explosions. Charlie Chaplin made 34 films in 34 weeks in 1914. Film comedy—wordless, zany, fast and free—delighted a wider audience than vaudeville had ever reached. Its generous humor, ranging from slapstick and satire to the new poetry of pathos created by Chaplin, included everyone. Children understood it, and immigrants, who had arrived by the millions, understood and enjoyed it too.

200,000 in New York City alone, one third of them children.

THE TRAMP, Charlie Chaplin's immortal creation, shuffles off at the end of a film. Chaplin introduced his famous outfit in 1914, in a film finished, the legend has it, in less than an hour.

Opera singers Lucien Muratore and Lina Cavalieri record a primitive wax cylinder. By 1910 the cylinders were being replaced by discs.

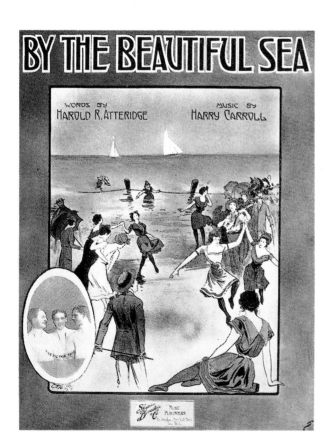

A POPULAR HIT of 1914 is Harry Carroll's "By the Beautiful Sea." Coney Island chorus boys dressed in sailor suits helped to promote this song's sheet-music sales throughout the country.

The rise and spread of popular music

THE new century had a new rhythm that was fast and jazzy. Movies were speeding up action, automobiles were speeding travel, and music, catching the tempo, turned from the placid waltz to the quickstepping ragtime. In the early 1900s black musicians had attracted crowds; soon their exciting syncopation was moving out of back rooms into popular dance halls as well as stately mansions. Ballroom dancing to such energetic steps as the bunny hug, the turkey trot or the grizzly bear became a nationwide fad. In 1910 the first dance marathon was held. Tin Pan Alley composers wrote music that could be both sung and danced to. In 1911, when Irving Berlin wrote "Everybody's Doin' It Now," what everybody was doing was the turkey trot. The new music was not only a rage on the dance floor; as sheet music it was also selling out. As many as a million copies of popular songs were snapped up. The phonograph, too, brought music into homes. Tinny but thrilling records played ragtime and, in that golden age of the opera, brought the greatest singers to enrapt listeners.

THE BOUNCY RAGTIME RHYTHM is celebrated in Irving Berlin's top tune of 1911. Songs had to have a danceable rhythm, and this one was just right for the turkey trot.

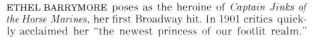

ETHEL BARRYMORE poses as the heroine of *Captain Jinks of the Horse Marines*, her first Broadway hit. In 1901 critics quickly acclaimed her "the newest princess of our footlit realm."

HARRY HOUDINI, master of escape, flexes his muscles before slipping out of chains, handcuffs and locks. After a slow start in vaudeville theaters, Houdini's tricks became world-famous.

The wider fame and larger fortunes of celebrities

FILMS, phonographs, and the vast vaudeville and theatrical circuits that linked the nation suddenly invested entertainers and artists with a new glamor. Their fame, like their audience, was no longer local but national, and even, occasionally, international. Acclaimed by millions, stars also made their millions. In record royalties alone, Caruso earned two million dol-

ENRICO CARUSO performs one of his noted roles, Don José in *Carmen*. After making his American debut in *Rigoletto* in 1903, Caruso sang for 17 seasons at the Metropolitan Opera.

MARY PICKFORD, America's Sweetheart, smiles her way to fortune. Sentimental in films, she was eminently practical off-camera, and by 1917 was earning nearly a million dollars a year.

lars. In movies the highest paid actors—Charlie Chaplin, Mary Pickford and Douglas Fairbanks—after having pushed their earnings close to the limit they could expect from producers, decided to pay themselves. In 1919 they formed their own company, United Artists. The shift in popularity of the stars had been swift. As late as 1913 few movies listed the names of their actors.

Soon, however, it was the stars, not the films, that attracted people. In the theater world, America's appetite for amusement was whetted and fed by syndicates: Klaw and Erlanger bossing a nationwide chain of theaters, Keith-Albee controlling most of vaudeville east of Chicago from 1905 to 1913. Entertainment, following the trend in other American activities, became big business.

4. THE SQUARE DEAL

W HEN the new century opened, the progressives had chieftains waging
localized battles but no national leader who could give inspiration
and direction to the group as a whole. Then, in September 1901, through the
unpredictable interposition of an assassin's bullet, Theodore Roosevelt succeeded William McKinley as President of the United States. Chance thus
placed in the highest office in the land a man with the bent and ability to
become the spokesman for a nationwide progressive movement.

Theodore Roosevelt's background resembled that of other campaigners for
government reform of the time. He came from an old family which, while still
well-to-do, was not rich by comparison with the new millionaires and captains
of industry. He had been taught from childhood to scorn mere money-making
and to value instead cultural pursuits and the dedication to public service.
He had also been brought up to believe that members of his social class were
the custodians of American traditions, the best judges of what was good for
the country. He had so much energy that Henry Adams once observed: "Roosevelt, more than any other man living . . . showed the singular primitive quality that belongs to ultimate matter—the quality that medieval theology as-
cribed to God—he was pure act."

Sickly as a child, he had conquered his infirmities by fierce exercise, and
in later life he boxed, played tennis, rode, hunted and hiked—all at an exhausting pace. He was no less energetic intellectually.

THEODORE ROOSEVELT appears somber in this portrait
by John Singer Sargent. The dynamic T. R.'s energetic
antitrust campaign was a highlight of the Progressive Era.

In March 1902 Roosevelt, the former "playboy of reform politics," launched an antitrust suit against the Northern Securities Company, a Morgan interest—the first of many such suits in the President's "moral crusade" against monopolies. This "Puck" cartoon, entitled "Bigger than his party," reflected the general conviction that T.R. was emerging as a powerful leader.

At Harvard he developed an abiding interest in history. Before graduating he began to write *The Naval War of 1812*, a study that remained standard for decades. Later he completed *The Winning of the West*, a classic account of the westward movement in the time of Daniel Boone. He was an omnivorous reader and a near-expert in half a dozen fields of social and natural science on which he wrote with skill and style.

Yet writing was not his principal trade. From first to last, his real occupation was politics. Before finishing his first book, young Roosevelt had told family friends that he "intended to be one of the governing class." To attain this end he learned the trade from the bottom. He was a member of the Republican Club in the New York City district where he lived. He served three terms in the state assembly, then ran unsuccessfully for mayor of New York. Through influential friends he secured appointive posts as Civil Service commissioner in Washington, as a member of the police commission in New York City (of which he was elected president), finally as Assistant Secretary of the Navy. After his triumphal return from Cuba in 1898, he was elected governor of New York. Then came the vice presidency and the fateful event that thrust him to the very top of the "governing class."

ALL the way up this ladder, his career had been marked by action. He had achieved prominence in the state legislature by forcing an investigation that leaders of neither party wanted, an investigation into corruption in the granting of a rapid transit franchise. As a police commissioner he roamed the streets at night, collaring delinquent patrolmen. He also brought down upon himself the wrath of the citizenry by enforcing ordinances requiring Sunday closing of saloons. In the Navy Department he loudly advocated greater preparedness and a more bellicose diplomacy. As governor he endorsed a program of corporate taxation that stirred furious debate.

Roosevelt was consistently theatrical, sometimes almost to the point of absurdity. In the 1880s, when he devoted part of his time to a ranch in the Dakotas, he affected ornate cowboy costumes. For his nighttime rounds as police commissioner he donned a black cloak and broad-brimmed hat. Even in the most sedate business dress, he had a touch of the stage about him, and his speech, when aroused, was high-pitched and usually loud. His smile was a startling, wide-mouthed display of incisors and canines "almost as big as colt's teeth"; his gestures were jerky and overemphatic; his stride was just short of a run. Some of his intimates thought of him as an overgrown boy.

On the other hand, if he was "about six," as one of his friends insisted, it did him little harm to be so. His mannerisms and displays were precisely those that made him good newspaper copy. No other New York City police commissioner could boast that his exploits had been written up in Baltimore and Chicago. No other colonel of volunteers netted as much publicity out of the short war in Cuba. Few other governors were so successful in appealing to the public to put pressure on recalcitrant legislators. No matter whether they found him amusing or infuriating or inspiring, people knew that Roosevelt would never be dull. They paid attention to him; this was to prove an invaluable asset in the presidency.

To his priceless endowments of talent, energy and popularity Roosevelt added another asset: From his scattered experiences in Albany, New York City and Washington, he had learned how to work the levers that made governmental machinery move. He understood the uses of patronage, of persuasion and flattery, of cajolery and pressure, and he had a superb sense of political timing. While he was a good historian, a capable writer, a well-rounded conversationalist and an admirable fighter, his greatness was as a politician.

In his first months in the White House, there was nothing in Roosevelt's behavior to alarm the conservatives. On taking office he told the press, "It shall be my aim to continue, absolutely unbroken, the policy of President McKinley for the peace, the prosperity, and the honor of our beloved country." He sent messages to Congress indistinguishable from McKinley's. Throughout the winter of 1901-1902, his only action at all out of the ordinary was his dinner invitation to Booker T. Washington, a distinguished educator who was head of the Tuskegee Institute and who happened to be a Negro. While this outraged white Southerners, it was in line with old-fashioned Republicanism.

Then in February 1902 Roosevelt suddenly made an attack on a great financial combination, J. P. Morgan's newly formed Northern Securities Company. The suit brought by the Attorney General charged that the company's control of three railroads made it a combination in restraint of interstate commerce and thus in violation of the Sherman Antitrust Act of 1890.

Taken by surprise, Morgan arranged to see the President at once. "If we have done anything wrong," said the financier, "send your man to my man and they can fix it up." To Morgan, "your man" was the Attorney General of the United States; "my man" was one of the Morgan lawyers. When told that the government wanted not to "fix it up" but to break up the Northern Securities Company, Morgan seemed nonplused. "Are you going to attack my other interests, the Steel Trust and the others?" he asked. "Certainly not," Roosevelt replied, "unless we find out that in any case they have done something that we regard as wrong."

Roosevelt remarked afterward that Morgan "could not help regarding me as a big rival operator, who either intended to ruin all his interests or else could be induced to come to an agreement to ruin none." He found this an amusing illustration of "the Wall Street point of view."

A cartoon take-off of "The Spirit of '76" shows T.R. as all three figures in the famous painting. The implication was that he planned to dominate the 1908 presidential campaign, and the publication commented: "If President Roosevelt hasn't told you by this time that under no circumstances will he accept a third term, it is a sign that you are not in his confidence."

IN a way, Morgan's attitude was justified. Since its enactment, the Sherman Act had been used chiefly to check labor-union activity. It had seldom been invoked against business. Indeed, the Supreme Court had declared it inapplicable to the case of the clear and unquestioned monopoly enjoyed by the sugar refiners. Roosevelt consulted with his Attorney General Philander Knox, who saw in the formation of the Northern Securities Company a violation of the act and buttressed Roosevelt's conviction that the multimillion dollar institution was not in the public interest. In his own fashion, T.R. was as arrogant as Morgan, and the Northern Securities suit was a first feint in a duel to determine which would be supreme—the White House on Pennsylvania Avenue in Washington or the House of Morgan at Broad and Wall Streets, New York City.

Moving with measured pace through the ordered hierarchy of the lower courts, the Northern Securities case was not decided by the Supreme Court until March 14, 1904. By that time Roosevelt was hopeful that the government's chances for a favorable decision might have been helped by the presence on the Court of the new justice he had named—Oliver Wendell Holmes, a leading advocate of more flexible constitutional interpretation. As it turned

Senator Thomas Platt, New York's Republican party boss, had helped elect T.R. governor, but later helped remove him from New York politics by nominating him for Vice President. However when T.R. succeeded to the presidency, Platt, as shown above, found "Teddy" missing from his shelf "for disobedient men."

Senator Matthew Stanley Quay of Pennsylvania was a hard-boiled machine politician, but he showed a touching concern for the long-suffering Delaware Indians. On his deathbed he asked Roosevelt to look after the tribe, and then expressed a wish to "crawl out on a rock in the sun and die like a wolf."

out, a far more important development had occurred: The continued crusading of the La Follettes and Tom Johnsons had helped to generate a change in the climate of opinion. Reinterpreting the Sherman Act, the Court ruled for the government, and the Northern Securities Company was dissolved. Mr. Justice Holmes, however, dissented.

Shortly after moving on the Northern Securities Company, Roosevelt had acted to break up the meat packers' trust. He then waited for the verdict in the Northern Securities case (and for further change in the climate of opinion) before opening a wholesale campaign against combinations. Although eventually he would press more than 40 antitrust suits, he was careful at first not to make it seem that he had declared war against big business.

The initiation of the Northern Securities and Beef Trust prosecutions was followed by a lull. Roosevelt turned his energies toward another of his many interests, conservation, and secured the passage of the Newlands Act (or Reclamation Act) in June 1902. This empowered the government to build dams and irrigation projects for the reclamation of arid lands in Western states. Meanwhile he delivered speeches calculated to soothe businessmen, as in the crisis caused by the anthracite coal strike. While Roosevelt held private discussions about the possibility of vigorous and perhaps unconstitutional action, such as seizure of the mines, he maintained a public appearance of a cautious, prudent middleman. Describing his role in the coal strikes, Roosevelt said that he sought a "square deal" for both capital and labor. His collaboration with Morgan in settling the strike was reassuring both to the financier and the business community at large.

ONCE the tremors caused by the Northern Securities suit had subsided (and the congressional elections of 1902 were over), Roosevelt made another startling move. He pressed Congress to enact two pieces of new legislation—one forbidding railroads to give rebates on freight charges, the other creating a Department of Commerce and Labor and, within it, a Bureau of Corporations empowered to investigate companies in interstate commerce.

The rebate measure arose out of demands from several groups: a substantial number of shippers, the railroads and the consumers. As Ida Tarbell was explaining in her McClure's articles, the Standard Oil Company had been able, because of the leverage of its immense volume of freight, to bargain with the railroads for a secret schedule of low rates. The difference between these and standard rates came back to Standard Oil in under-the-counter rebates, while competitors paid the standard charges in full. For a time, Standard Oil even got rebates on the charges paid by its competitors. Under such conditions, the oil trust could always undersell everybody else. This was one reason why competition had been killed off.

Rebating had spread to other industries and had become so complex in certain industries that there existed sliding scales of rebates. Robert La Follette later told of a Wisconsin manufacturer who had been pleased with a secret rebate of 50 cents out of every $1.50 he paid until he discovered that his chief rivals were getting back 65 cents. In disgust, many businessmen concluded that it would be better if all rebates were stopped. Harassed railroad executives heartily agreed.

For this reason Roosevelt's demand for an end to rebates could have expected to meet opposition only from spokesmen for gigantic concerns such as Standard Oil, even in that era when the Senate was called the "Millionaires' Club." A rich, very conservative Republican, Senator Stephen B. Elkins of West Virginia, introduced the measure and it quickly passed.

The proposed department and bureau received quite a different response. Large numbers of businessmen were extremely dubious about allowing any governmental agency to pry into their affairs. In both houses of Congress blocs of conservatives formed to fight the President. Although these opposition groups were in the minority, the question remained whether the majority on the President's side would insist on affirmative action.

ROOSEVELT judged that Congress needed some evidence that the voters really wanted the measure. He took the occasion, therefore, to tell reporters in confidence that John D. Rockefeller had wired various senators urging them to oppose the creation of the new department and bureau. Ida Tarbell's articles were then attracting nationwide attention, and this fresh information of Standard Oil's tactics became front-page news. Implicated congressmen screamed indignant denials, but these were countered by disclosure of the fact that the accusation had come from none other than the President. The story stayed in the headlines.

From all over the country, legislators heard from constituents concerned about the sinister influence that Rockefeller might be exerting. The bill was hastily brought up and passed almost without recorded opposition.

The index of Roosevelt's eagerness to win this fight is found in his resort to propaganda, for, as he probably knew, it was not Rockefeller who had sent the messages. Telegrams had been sent, but they had come from Standard Oil's chief counsel, John D. Archbold. Roosevelt had substituted Rockefeller's name because it had much greater news value. He had played a trick, and it had worked. On February 19, 1903, Roosevelt was gleeful: his package of antitrust measures—the Elkins Act, the Department of Commerce and Labor measure and the Expedition Act (which speeded prosecution of cases against combinations)—all became law on that day.

Significantly, Roosevelt had managed to win without humiliating or embittering those who opposed him. Using his powers of persuasion, he convinced Republican leaders that they had nothing further to fear. And by agreement with Nelson W. Aldrich of Rhode Island, the most powerful of the Senate conservatives, he had Attorney General Knox announce that "Congress has now enacted all that is practicable and all that is desirable to do."

Through 1903 and most of 1904, Roosevelt said almost nothing that could be interpreted as radical. He and his very capable Secretary of War, Elihu Root, conducted a campaign for administrative reform of the Army, culminating in the creation of a general staff, the consolidation of the unwieldy services of supply into one department and improvement in organization and training of the National Guard.

The military reforms met opposition from Army traditionalists, and T.R.'s victory supplied further proof of his popularity and political skill. But it did not bring him into conflict with the titans of business or their congressional spokesmen. Meanwhile he took occasion to write Morgan and others, asking their advice about future policies and legislation.

Roosevelt was as yet no more than a mild progressive. But he had established himself as a leader. Except for Cleveland, all his predecessors from

As Speaker of the House during Roosevelt's Administration, "Uncle Joe" Cannon pushed T.R.'s program when it conformed to the ideas of the Republican Old Guard. But he often opposed T.R., once declaring that he was "tired of listening to all this babble for reform . . . America is a hell of a success."

Stephen Elkins—caricatured by Thomas Fleming, as were the others on these pages—was in the Senate when T.R. put pressure on those who represented big business. Elkins bemoaned his wealth: "Very rich men never whistle, poor men always do; bird songs are in the hearts of the people."

Grant on had been faithful Republicans, content to be led by Congress or the party bosses. Cleveland had been, for the most part, a negative President, merely blocking congressional action of which he disapproved. Roosevelt had shown that he meant to formulate programs of his own and bend the legislative branch to his will. He was setting a new pattern in the presidency.

Roosevelt had a larger program in mind, but first he had to win a second term. Through 1903 and even into 1904 he manifested one of his few out-of-character traits—an almost hysterical fear of defeat at the convention. Mark Hanna was a possible rival, for Hanna's name aroused much more enthusiasm among businessmen than did Roosevelt's, and Hanna had a strong network of alliances with prospective delegates to the national convention. Hanna's sudden death from typhoid fever in February 1904 gave Roosevelt the final assurance that he would be the G.O.P.'s choice.

There remained the election itself. To oppose him the Democrats nominated Judge Alton B. Parker of the New York Court of Appeals. An unimaginative man who opposed government interference with "natural" economic processes, Parker was clearly the more conservative candidate. Nonetheless Republican lines held firm, and T.R.'s Secretary of Commerce and Labor, George B. Cortelyou, was able to solicit huge campaign contributions from the business community.

Though Roosevelt guarded his words, avoided issues and observed the convention that an incumbent President running for re-election do little active campaigning, the fact that the Republican was the liberal and the Democrat the conservative became more and more apparent. By election day the choice for the voter who wanted to preserve the status quo seemed to be Parker rather than Roosevelt.

Roosevelt won with 7,628,461 votes to Parker's 5,084,223. This was the largest percentage of the popular vote achieved in American history up to that time and an unusually large majority of 196 in electoral votes. The voters appeared to have spoken for reform.

Submarine designer John Holland emerges from the "Holland," which in 1900 became the first underwater craft accepted by the U.S. Navy. An Irish immigrant, Holland had built his first sub with funds from the Fenian Society. This group of American-based Irish patriots had made its contributions for one reason: to develop a craft capable of sinking the whole English fleet.

Now that he was assured of four more years in which to pursue his goals, Roosevelt was less hesitant about speaking out. Addressing the Union League Club of Philadelphia in January 1905, the President sounded the keynote of the program that had been maturing in his mind and to which he was to direct his energies during his second term.

> Unquestionably . . . the great development of industrialism means that there must be an increase in the supervision exercised by the Government over business enterprises. . . . Neither this people nor any other free people will permanently tolerate the use of the vast power conferred by vast wealth, and especially by wealth in its corporate form, without lodging somewhere in the Government the still higher power of seeing that this power, in addition to being used in the interest of the individual or individuals possessing it, is also used for and not against the interests of the people as a whole. . . . No finally satisfactory result can be expected from merely State action. The action must come through the Federal Government.

The first specific measure Roosevelt called for was effective federal regulation of railroad freight rates. This was not a new idea. On the state level it had been advocated by Grangers and Populists long before the progressive movement had crystallized. A number of state railroad commissions had been created from the late '70s onward. In 1887 Congress had established an Interstate Commerce Commission to supervise rate making. But railroad lawyers had battled all these agencies, persuaded the courts to chip away their powers and rendered regulation practically ineffectual. The I.C.C., in practice, could secure only a limited amount of information from the companies; its orders did not have to be obeyed, and, if it wanted to force a change in a rate, it had to bring suit in a federal court, hoping that after a few years it might win its case. What Roosevelt proposed was that the 1887 law be tightened, that the commission be given the power to establish ceilings on freight rates and that its decrees should receive the force of law.

Conservatives found these proposals alarming. Railroading was one of the biggest and most powerful businesses in the country, and it was the industry in which most of the great financial moguls were involved. Most conservatives fervently asserted that it was morally wrong for government to dictate how owners of property should use their property—the argument made by railroad lawyers to undermine the earlier laws. Conservatives, moreover, were fearful that public opinion might support Roosevelt and force Congress to accept the measure.

Financial leaders got in touch with congressmen, urging them to stand fast against any new regulatory law. Working from the other direction, a worried conservative in the House of Representatives, Joseph C. Sibley of Pennsylvania, wrote to John Archbold of Standard Oil urgently recommending that the big corporations join forces to establish a propaganda bureau, get "permanent and healthy control of the Associated Press and other kindred avenues," and thus create a publicity machine that could oppose the movement toward government interference with business.

Roosevelt was ready for a battle. Before making the Union League speech, he had consulted quietly with congressional leaders and learned the extent of the opposition he might expect in the House and in the Senate. He was careful, therefore, to recommend that the I.C.C. be given the power to fix rates only after hearing complaints from shippers that particular charges were unfair. The establishment of a judicial or quasi-judicial procedure, he thought, would seem less socialistic than if the commission were given the right to set rates on its own initiative.

It took the public nearly five years to recognize the importance of the Wright brothers' historic flight at Kitty Hawk in 1903 (below). Then these two reticent men were showered with acclaim. Once, after enduring many long-winded speeches at a dinner, Wilbur broke his customary silence, saying: "The most talkative bird in the world is the parrot. But he is a poor flyer."

WHITE HOUSE
WASHINGTON *June 22d*
1904

Darling Ethel,
Here goes for the
picture letter!

Ethel administers necessary
discipline to Archie and
Quentin.

Ethel gives sick Yagenka
a bottle of medicine

Father plays tennis
with Mr. Cooley. ———

Leo chases a squirrel
which fortunately he can't catch

A nice policeman feeding
a squirrel with bread;
I fed two with bread
this afternoon.

This note, illustrated by T.R., is
one of the many letters that Roose-
velt wrote to his children. It was
written to his daughter Ethel when
she was 12. Because Ethel had been
something of a tomboy as a child,
her father called her "Elephant
Johnnie." Other family recollec-
tions had Ethel eating a toadstool
and gulping some potassium ni-
trate with no harmful aftereffects.

By the spring of 1905 T.R. knew that he could carry such a plan through the House. He had taken care to make a deal with Speaker Joseph Cannon, whose power to control the flow of legislation in the House was then formidable. "Uncle Joe" had stronger feelings about the tariff than about any other issues, so Roosevelt had dropped hints that he was thinking of proposing tariff cuts. Privately, T.R. agreed with the Speaker that it was wisest to leave the tariff alone. Roosevelt felt that even an inconclusive debate on the tariff could provoke financial unrest or cause a split in the Republican party. The President's hints laid the basis for a meeting with Cannon at the White House to work out a compromise. By promising not to advocate major changes in the tariff, Roosevelt obtained a *quid pro quo* from the Speaker in the form of a pledge of support for the railroad rate measures. Now it was certain that the I.C.C. bill would pass the House.

The real arena of battle was, therefore, the Senate. Unlike the House, it had no czar. Insofar as the senators accepted any leadership at all, they took it from a handful of men, all of whom were veterans of a decade or more in Congress and nearly all of whom were known for their close connections with great industrialists and financiers. Aware of progressive tides in their home states, some of these leaders were ready to support Roosevelt's bill. Others were determined to fight it. Among these was the ablest and most influential senator, Nelson W. Aldrich.

TALL, alert, a man of imperturbable dignity, Aldrich seemed an aristocrat to the bone. In fact he had started as a delivery boy and made a fortune in the dog-eat-dog business of manipulating streetcar franchises. But all outward traces of this past had vanished. He was now a man who yachted with J. Pierpont Morgan and whose son-in-law was John D. Rockefeller Jr. All that remained of the career that had made him a multimillionaire were certain techniques that, refined, had application in the Senate: the persuasiveness and charm of a master salesman; the quickness of mind of a man whose basic tenet was that opportunity knocks but once; the craftiness of a manipulator who measured his opponents, credited them with maximum skill, and still outthought them. He was a formidable foe.

When Roosevelt's rate-regulation measure, the Hepburn bill, cleared the House and came to the Senate, Aldrich no longer had the power to muster a majority against it. The Democrats, La Follette and a few other progressive Republicans in the Senate had been joined by a number of conservative Republicans who had become so fearful of the progressive movement that they were willing to make compromises. The question was whether Aldrich could delay the bill's coming to a vote or, alternatively, nullify it through the addition of amendments.

The 13 members of the Committee on Interstate and Foreign Commerce sat to consider the measure the House had passed. Five were Democrats, eight Republicans. Aldrich had a majority of the latter with him, though three of the Republicans were prepared to vote with the Democrats to defeat any crippling amendments. Their plan was to fight Aldrich in committee as allies of the Democrats. When the bill reached the floor, however, they proposed to treat it as an administration or party measure, deserving support from the Republican majority.

In the committee room the bipartisan opposition waited expectantly for

Aldrich's amendments. Provision after provision came up without the Rhode Islander proposing changes. Normally quiet and soft-spoken, he now sat at the table in almost Buddha-like calm. The three Republicans who had been anticipating a battle concluded that he was accepting defeat gracefully.

In fact, however, he was busily holding conferences with some of the Democratic committeemen in the intervals between committee sessions. When the bill was almost in final form, Aldrich put forward a motion. Ordinarily, a majority report of a committee carried with it a guarantee of support in the floor debate by all majority members of the committee. Aldrich now proposed that individual members of the committee be permitted to introduce amendments on the floor. To the consternation of Roosevelt's supporters, this resolution passed. It now became evident that the battle had just begun.

Aldrich quickly struck a second blow, this one even more guileful. One of the Republicans backing the bill had expected, as a matter of course, to be named to manage the debate in the Senate. Instead, the committee chose a Democrat, "Pitchfork Ben" Tillman of South Carolina, a former Populist who was in favor of the bill but who was not on speaking terms with T.R. The whole strategy of the Administration faction was undone. Not only would there be open fighting over amendments, but the original bill could no longer be represented as a Republican party measure. Deftly turning disadvantage into advantage, Aldrich had gained the upper hand.

Days of maneuver followed. When debate opened in the Senate, the Administration forces tried to forge a coalition of Bryan Democrats, progressives and regular Republicans. The President moved toward the somewhat more radical position taken by the Democrats. But Tillman was unable to carry his party with him. And the concessions that T.R. made to Tillman had cost him Republican votes. In congressional cloakrooms the consensus was that in the final test Aldrich would be the victor, Roosevelt the loser.

Before the decisive moment arrived, however, something happened. Neither the scanty papers left by Aldrich nor the voluminous Roosevelt memorabilia provide any relevant evidence. Only the result is on the record. The senator and the President somehow came to an agreement. Roosevelt backed away from the extreme position into which he had edged. Aldrich in return let the Senate pass the Hepburn bill in May 1906 virtually as it had come from the House, adding no crippling amendments.

Roosevelt's enthusiasm for simplified spelling, lampooned in the cartoon above, led him to order the Public Printer to spell some 300 words according to rules drawn up by the Simplified Spelling Board, a private group. A storm of criticism soon forced T.R. to rescind the order, but not before his Secretary of State, Elihu Root, had twitted him with the note reproduced below.

DEPARTMENT OF STATE,
WASHINGTON.

Dere Theodor Pleas rede this thru + giv it bak Er. [Root]

PERHAPS Aldrich counted on the courts to hamstring rate regulation. Perhaps as the battle progressed he concluded that he did not really want a victory—that the long-term interests of business were more likely to be served if Roosevelt was not driven into permanent alliance with such men as Tillman and La Follette. While Aldrich was a conservative to the depths of his being, he had that wisdom that has been the salvation of conservatism in America and England. Recognizing change to be inevitable, he regarded it his duty to slow progress down rather than fight it, and he may well have compromised in this instance because he realized that a triumph would not last and that all too soon, other, perhaps more important, occasions for delaying action would arise.

This was to be the case. The future would bring far more serious efforts to impose controls on business. Nevertheless the passage of the Hepburn Act does seem to have been a turning point. For the first time an agency of the federal government was to have real power over an industry—power to inspect company books, power to issue orders to great companies, power to fix maximum freight rates. This law gave a clear indication that there was in America a force—the federal government—that could cope with great concentrations of private economic might.

After the passage of the Hepburn Act, Roosevelt lost none of his energy. Although he was unwilling to go as far as some reformers would, he did respond to public concern over muckrakers' revelations about the meat-packing and patent-medicine industries by sponsoring the Pure Food and Drug Act. To avoid another all-out fight, T.R. permitted certain of the stronger provisions to be revised or deleted, but the government got some power to set standards for processed foods and pharmaceuticals.

In 1907 Roosevelt executed an adroit end-run to frustrate opponents of conservation. His chief forester Gifford Pinchot had been steadily enlarging the federal forest preserves, to the annoyance of timber companies and land speculators. Western congressmen tacked onto an appropriation bill an amendment forbidding Pinchot to continue this work in certain states. Roosevelt felt he could not veto the bill, but he withheld signing it for the full 10 days permitted by the Constitution. Meanwhile he proclaimed 21 new areas as preserves, totaling 16 million acres. Subsequently he began an intensive campaign to educate the public about conservation. He had little influence on Congress, but he did succeed in making enough converts among governors that soon there were conservation commissions in the majority of states.

Roosevelt kept himself in the public eye, often by riding one hobby or another. He became embroiled with writers of sentimentalized animal books, whom he denounced as "nature-fakers." He lost ground in this battle after one of the nature-fakers retorted that whenever the President "gets near the heart of a wild thing, he invariably puts a bullet through it." His attempt to impose simplified spelling was another fiasco.

In the midst of these frivolous controversies, he became involved in a more serious dispute. On the basis of a report that Negro soldiers had been responsible for a midnight riot at Brownsville, Texas, Roosevelt ordered dishonorable discharges for almost every soldier in three entire companies allegedly involved in the incident. An Ohio Senator, Joseph B. Foraker, after examining the evidence, accused the President of having acted impulsively and unfairly. Roosevelt defended himself vigorously but in the end had to admit, at least by implication, that he had done wrong. He arranged for hearings that resulted in reinstatement of some of the men.

These episodes dissipated some of Roosevelt's popularity and strength. More costly to him still was the Panic of 1907, for many businessmen blamed it on the Hepburn Act, saying that investors and depositors had been frightened by government interference with the profit system. Since many voters accepted this explanation, Congress temporarily became an inhospitable place for reform proposals.

In previous utterances Roosevelt had expressed scorn for people who put forward utopian projects instead of concentrating on the practical and attainable. Now, however, he seemed to change his mind. Perhaps because he could see no hope of even modest legislative accomplishments during the

A newspaper cartoon, in which Uncle Sam endorses Roosevelt with the words "He's good enough for me" (above), played an important part in the 1904 campaign. It was both widely hailed and widely criticized. Frederick Opper, cartoonist for the opposition Hearst newspapers, for example, countered with a parody (below) in which his familiar figure of "The Trusts" replaced Uncle Sam.

time that remained of his presidency (in 1904 he had promised not to run for another term), he began to advance ideas that were realizable only in the distant future, if at all.

Between 1907 and 1909 he recommended federal inheritance and income taxes, the eight-hour day·for workers and compulsory investigation of major labor disputes; he asked that corporations engaged in interstate commerce be required to obtain federal licenses; and, expressing outrage at "malefactors of great wealth," he proposed that antitrust violations, as well as unfair labor practices and stock-market manipulations, be made crimes punishable by prison sentences.

The cautious projects that he had earlier put forward and translated into law—the ban on rebates, railroad rate regulation, and food and drug inspection—had been criticized by La Follette and other progressives as halfway measures. The obvious answer had been that they were all Congress and the public would accept. But after 1907 Roosevelt was proposing even more far-reaching business reforms than had been adopted in some of the states where progressives were in power.

Roosevelt did not say that bigness in business was inherently bad. Indeed, he implied that if it made for greater efficiency, lower unit cost and better distribution, it was to the good. But as a check on the power of great corporations, he advocated a bigger and more powerful federal government—one that, in the name of the public, would tell business not only what it could not do but what it *should* do.

Others had arrived at the same idea. One was George W. Perkins, a Morgan partner interested in public affairs. Another was Herbert Croly, a journalist who would soon set forth a systematic program of reform in *The Promise of American Life*. But Roosevelt's concepts were sufficiently ahead of their time that they were not generally understood. Indeed, the implications of what Roosevelt said in 1908 and 1909 were so little appreciated then that when he reiterated the same theories later on, some people thought he had been inspired by Croly.

A lethargic campaigner, William Howard Taft was pushed toward the presidency in 1908 by the outgoing Roosevelt and won by a slim popular margin. The English magazine "Punch" ran this cartoon showing Taft being carried over the election hurdles while clinging to the old Rough Rider's stirrup. Its title—"Alone I didn't do it" —was devastatingly accurate.

IN the early 1900s most Americans worried by industrialization were longing for ways of restoring the past—of re-creating a society in which small farmers and small businessmen predominated. Discarding such dreams, Roosevelt was asserting that the concentration of economic power had come to stay, that the future lay with big organizations who would hold the little men, whether farmer, businessman or consumer, at their mercy unless the biggest organization of all were a government responsive to the public will.

Roosevelt preached these ideas vigorously as long as he retained the White House as a forum. Whatever inner feelings he may have had, in 1908 he regarded himself as bound by his pledge not to run again. After considering a number of other possible candidates, he selected Secretary of War William Howard Taft as his successor; when Taft had been nominated and elected and inaugurated, Roosevelt cheerfully turned over his office and departed for a hunting trip in Africa. He may well have been content with having written a few new laws and to have ended his presidency anticipating a future that was sure to materialize. Or perhaps he recognized, at least subconsciously, that he was only 50 and that if in time the people saw the wisdom of his visions, a call might come again for him to serve the republic.

Unaware of the imminent change in his life, T.R. (center) faces reporters on the day McKinley was shot.

Teddy Roosevelt's strenuous lives

THE 60 crowded years of Theodore Roosevelt's life saw the United States transformed. When he was born on October 27, 1858, the Civil War was still a dread menace that men of good will hoped could be averted, and America a country preoccupied with itself. When he died on January 6, 1919, the First World War was a nightmare the country had fought through to victory, and America was irrevocably a world power. At home a tremendous industrial expansion had taken place; to match it the powers of government had grown with almost equal speed. Vigorously participating in many of these changes was the ever-ebullient T.R. The painting opposite suggests a few of his enthusiasms and achievements. Above his forcefully smiling portrait is a battleship, a reminder of the Great White Fleet he sent around the world in 1907 as a token of American power. Clockwise, starting below, are a brooch showing him as a Rough Rider in the Spanish-American War, a cartoon tribute to his role in building the Panama Canal, a souvenir from the Bull Moose presidential fight of 1912, the Nobel Peace Prize medal he won in 1906 for mediating the Russo-Japanese War and a 1904 campaign button recording his pledge of a "square deal" for everyone. The gnarled bludgeon stands for his political philosophy: "Speak softly and carry a big stick."

The full impact of T.R.'s incredible energy might never have been felt had McKinley recovered from the assassin's bullet in 1901. Roosevelt, deep in the Adirondacks when news of the death reached him, rattled by wagon down the trail to Buffalo and the White House, crying: "Go ahead, go on, go on."

T.R. TRADEMARKS, his glittering teeth and flashing spectacles, dominate a still life of Roosevelt memorabilia and portrait. This portrait is based on a 1912 photograph.

"I TOOK THE ISTHMUS"

A SQUARE DEAL ALL AROUND

T.R.

PRO PACE ET FRATERNITA

NEW YORK · U.S. 66

T.R., trounced when he ran for mayor

STAGILY CLAD in fringed buckskins, Roosevelt helps to promote his book about Western hunting. One tale had him shooting a panther as he hung upside down over the edge of a cliff.

SPORTING A BEARD, Harvard boxer T.R. glowers. He thought Yale men "a much more scrubby set than ours."

of New York, is ridiculed as a future candidate in this 1887 cartoon. But T. R. later convinced Republican bosses that he could be a winner.

A wealthy young man's burning compulsion to excel

T. R. was a sickly child, asthmatic and nearsighted. When his father, a successful New York merchant, told him his body would never allow him a useful career, he answered, "I'll make my body." And he did, with a rush of energy that never let up. Once he played 91 games of tennis in a day. Fresh out of Harvard (where he had begun to write the first of his many books, *The Naval War of 1812*), he married Alice Lee, daughter of Boston Brahmins; during a belated honeymoon he took time out to climb the Matterhorn in the Alps. Returned home, he plunged into politics as a New York state assemblyman. When Alice died in childbirth, he worked off his grief as a rancher in North Dakota, even becoming a deputy sheriff. ("My trip down the river after the three thieves was a grand success," he wrote to his sister.) In later years T.R. reminisced: "There were all kinds of things of which I was afraid at first . . . but by acting as if I was not afraid I gradually ceased to be afraid."

BRIMFUL OF PRIDE, T.R. holds baby Archibald. In this 1894 photo Edith, T.R.'s second wife, clasps Kermit and Ethel; Theodore, Jr. and Alice, daughter of his first wife, stand behind.

Roosevelt is seen above in six campaign poses that roused voters across the nation. A contemporary described his style: "His teeth snap

Roosevelt the popular Rough Rider dwarfs President McKinley in this 1900 cartoon, just as he did in the eyes of many Americans.

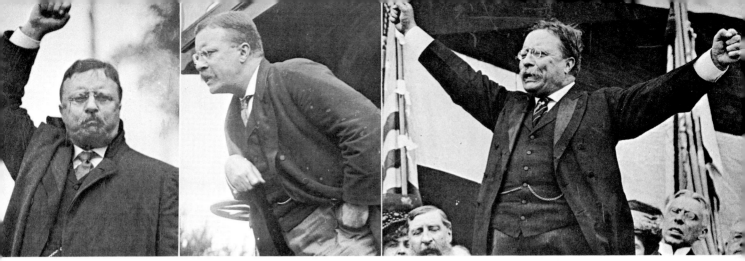

shut between the syllables, biting them apart . . . a sharp forward thrust of the head . . . seems to throw the word clattering into the air."

The stormy Administration of a strong President

As President, T.R. outraged the Old Guard Republican party bosses who thought that they had silenced this magnetic Spanish-American War hero by nominating him as McKinley's Vice President. Once in office, T.R. gathered to the peacetime presidency more power than it ever had held. A British visitor wrote that Roosevelt was a mixture "of St. Vitus and St. Paul." A vital, trust-busting, strike-mediating President, he sought to protect the public against what he once called the twin evils of "government by a plutocracy and . . . by a mob." Grateful voters voiced their approval by a landslide in 1904. Despite this vote of confidence, Congress gave him trouble. When it passed bills he disliked, he signed them with a scrawled "T. Roosevelt" instead of his full name. Nevertheless toward the end of his term he crowed: "I have had a great time as President."

His head arrogantly thrown back, T.R. is shown as a conquering Caesar after the 1904 election. Trailing him are disgruntled politicians.

PLAYING ENGINEER, T.R. takes the controls of a giant steam shovel during his inspection of the Panama Canal in 1906. He checked into everything, including the price of yams, and wrote home: "I tramped everywhere through the mud." Later he would dismiss charges of "imperialism" in dealing with Panama by saying: "I took the Canal Zone and let Congress debate."

In Florida T.R. and a friend show off the devilfish the ex-President harpooned.

In Africa Roosevelt displays a rhino and a bustard.

In the Sudan, T.R. and a live animal!

In Brazil Roosevelt's party descends the desolate River of Doubt in the Amazon wilderness.

Within the man,
a ceaselessly wandering boy

HORSEBACK HARANGUE engages Wilhelm II, who signed this picture: "The argument driven home!" Roosevelt said he had once used the threat of the U.S. fleet to check German schemes.

FROM childhood, when he toured Europe and Egypt with his parents, Teddy Roosevelt had wanderlust. While President he visited America's cities, hunted insatiably in its wilds (causing Mark Twain to joke that one of his targets was a cow, not a bear), inspected waterways (being thrown through a window when his riverboat collided with another), went down in a submarine (insisting on steering) and toured the Panama Canal diggings (*opposite*). In 1909, out of office, he sailed for a year of hunting in Africa, where he assembled what was probably the largest collection of African fauna then known. He went on to a glorious tour of Europe that included riding with Kaiser Wilhelm II of Germany (*right*) and lecturing at Oxford and the Sorbonne—at the latter in execrable French. His last great journey was a voyage down a tributary of the Amazon in 1913-1914. The fever he contracted there destroyed his health. "I had to go," he said. "It was my last chance to be a boy."

A FIERCE CARTOON ATTACK recalls Roosevelt's presidential campaign in 1912. Never modest, he once praised himself as "better fitted to do the job than anyone else." To assaults on his conduct in office, he had said: "I feel we are certainly justified in morals, and therefore . . . in law." Still he asked a friend: "Why, why is it that I arouse so much animosity?"

A youthful elder statesman frustrated by defeat

THE presidential campaign of 1912 was a four-way race: Roosevelt, attempting a comeback on the Bull Moose ticket, was pitted against the Republicans' William Howard Taft, the Democrats' Woodrow Wilson and the Socialists' Eugene Debs. Taft had been hand-picked by Roosevelt as his successor four years before; now T.R. felt that Taft had sold out to the Old Guard. "We stand at Armageddon and we battle for the Lord," T.R. had cried, but the struggle was fought on an earthier level. Roosevelt excoriated Taft as a "fathead" with "brains less than those of a guinea pig." Taft called T.R. "a dangerous egotist" and "demagogue." In Milwaukee a man named John Schrank shot Roosevelt on his way to deliver a speech. The manuscript in his breast pocket slowed the bullet, and T.R. went ahead and gave his address, showing the crowd his bloody shirt and punctured text. "On account of my broken rib . . . I could not speak as loudly as usual," was his chief complaint. But he lost the election: a split vote gave Wilson the victory.

AS THE BULL MOOSE CANDIDATE Roosevelt speaks to a meeting in Morrisville, Vermont. His Progressive party took its nickname from T.R.'s remark: "I am as strong as a bull moose."

His offer to raise World War I troops spurned by President Wilson, T.R. busies himself by contributing to a Girl Scout scrap-metal drive.

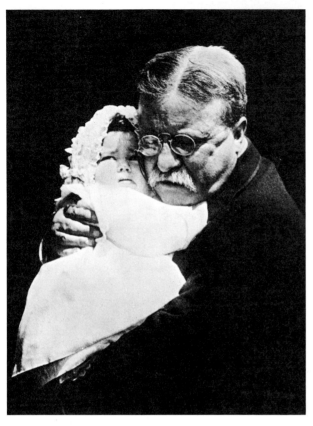

A DOTING ROOSEVELT hugs a grandchild. Early one morning he alarmed house guests by pounding on their door to show them "a baby's hand . . . the most beautiful thing in the world."

A loving man and a living monument

A FAMILY man quite as much as a public figure, Roosevelt for more than 30 years centered his life around Sagamore Hill, his home at Oyster Bay on Long Island, New York. The North Room (*opposite*) is filled with reminders of his public life. The elephant tusks were a gift from the Emperor of Abyssinia; the carpet, from the Shah of Persia. In a glass case on the table of Philippine mahogany is a model of a suit of Japanese armor presented by Admiral Togo, a naval hero of the Russo-Japanese War. But in this house, too, T.R. raised his six children. Often he took them—and startled house guests—on breakneck cross-country hikes. Here he lived out his last years, blind in one eye from a boxing accident, rocking his grandchildren in a chair on the shady porch while loyal supporters called to urge him to return to politics. Here, finally, T.R. died in his sleep one January night in 1919. Today Sagamore Hill is a museum, visited every year by some 60,000 people. The spirit of "the old lion," as his boys called him, still fills its rooms.

The North Room at Sagamore Hill is pure T.R. Before an alcove

of books (left) stands a St. Gaudens bronze, "The Puritan," that contrasts with hunting trophies. On the far wall is his presidential flag.

5. THE
TRIUMPH OF
PROGRESSIVISM

THE man who became President on March 4, 1909, was clearly ill-suited to the task of advancing Roosevelt's program. Good-natured, easygoing, grotesquely overweight, William Howard Taft had really wanted to be a judge. Only because of the proddings of an ambitious wife had he accepted the succession of executive appointments that led him to the presidency. Though he had served capably in these posts, he had little experience in elective politics to make up for his lack of drive and imagination. In an unwitting suggestion of his own self-doubts, Taft once remarked that whenever someone said "Mr. President," he looked around for Roosevelt.

Yet Taft earnestly wished to take up where his predecessor left off. His intention was to press on Congress the measures that Roosevelt had advocated in 1907 and 1908. Since the elections of 1908 had added to the number of progressive Republicans in Congress, there was reason to hope that at least some bills might pass. Unhappily, Taft lost no time in showing his political naiveté. For his first test of strength on Capitol Hill he chose an extremely delicate and complicated issue—the tariff.

Taft had some good luck at the outset. Speaker of the House Joe Cannon, an old and fervent enemy of tariff reforms, had a battle on his hands. A group of the progressive, "insurgent" Republicans were threatening to unite with Democrats and rewrite the House rules to end "Cannonism"—that is, to reduce the Speaker's vast powers to control the progress of legislation. "Uncle

ROOSEVELT'S ROTUND SUCCESSOR, William Howard Taft, betrays none of his predecessor's verve, but his Administration's reform record was remarkably impressive.

This 1902 caricature contrasts two Democratic congressmen, Oliver H.P. Belmont of New York and Champ Clark of Missouri. Belmont, said the caption, required "four words to fully express his name; but . . . double as many figures to indicate his fortune." Clark kept his fortune beneath his hat —"inasmuch as his mind is a perfect mine of oratorical wealth."

Joe" was so worried by this coalition that he was willing to make a deal. If the President would use his influence to frustrate the reform movement, Cannon would work to push an Administration tariff bill through the House. Taft, by accepting this bargain, got the tariff legislation halfway to enactment.

In the Senate, however, Republican leader Nelson Aldrich mustered votes from both parties to pass amendments jacking rates back up and nullifying many of the reforms Taft wanted. By the time a conference committee was set up to reconcile the House and Senate versions, Cannon, temporarily out of danger, appointed to it representatives who favored the high-tariff Senate draft. The President seemed to have been beaten.

Taft fought back and managed to recover something. The progressives and a number of Democrats had advocated a small personal income tax to make up the revenue that would be lost if duties were lowered. The Supreme Court had ruled such a tax unconstitutional in 1895, but the reform coalition seemed strong enough to pass an amendment to the tariff bill that would authorize the tax. Taft warned the Republican Old Guard of the possibility, advocating a corporation income tax instead. The corporate tax was passed in the Senate, and the conference committee retained it in the final act, which the President justified as "a revision substantially downward." Actually the act kept high tariff levels for most manufactured goods and lowered protection on many raw materials produced in the South and Middle West. At first Taft escaped most of the criticism of the new tariff. But at Winona, Minnesota, he made the bad mistake of describing it as "the best bill that the Republican party ever passed." At this the Middle West rose up in arms against him.

Whatever prestige Taft had salvaged in the tariff battle was undone by harsh recriminations. Progressives found it hard to forgive Taft for backing Cannon in the House, for agreeing to compromises with Aldrich and for giving up the project of an immediate personal income tax law. These men, feeling that they had been betrayed, criticized the President loudly and harshly. Roosevelt—who understood the progressives—had borne their attacks, wooed them back and kept them as allies. Taft had no such tact or restraint. Stung by the reform group's attacks, he retaliated with snubs and other signs of displeasure. As his relations with the progressives worsened, he found himself aligned more and more closely with the conservatives.

THE Ballinger-Pinchot affair widened the split between Taft and the progressives. A Land Office investigator, Louis R. Glavis, had turned up evidence implicating Taft's Secretary of the Interior, Richard Ballinger, in a questionable Alaskan land deal. When Glavis became convinced that his superiors meant to stop further investigation, he took his report to Chief Forester Pinchot, whom he knew to be both an ardent conservationist and a foe of Ballinger. Pinchot passed it on to Taft. Since the data seemed inconclusive to Taft, he judged the charges to be malicious and ordered Glavis fired.

Pinchot then jumped to the conclusion that Taft was covering up for Ballinger. Glavis, with Pinchot's help, prepared some sensational articles which were published in Collier's magazine, and the public let loose a roar of indignation. Pinchot went on to stir up congressional attacks on Ballinger. When these activities came to light, Taft fired Pinchot.

Congressional progressives instantly took Pinchot's side and charged Taft with being an enemy of conservation. Although a special House-Senate investigation exonerated both Ballinger and Taft of charges of fraud and corruption, the progressives remained unconvinced. The vilification that they heaped on the President made any future reconciliation all but impossible.

Meanwhile the power of the progressives mounted. In the House, the so-called "insurgents" were already caucusing separately and negotiating with the Democratic minority about the project nearest their hearts—the overthrow of Cannon. In March 1910, while excitement over the Pinchot case still raged, they sallied into battle again.

Cannon himself inadvertently gave them their opening. Ruling on a routine measure affecting the census, he said that it could be brought to the floor out of parliamentary order because it had to do with an area of legislation specifically mentioned in the Constitution. Representative George Norris of Nebraska rose. For two years this quiet, intense insurgent Republican had been carrying around in his pocket a draft resolution that called for fundamental changes in the procedures of the House. In the past he had been unable to get it to the floor. Now, however, on the same principle that applied to the census measure, Norris demanded that his resolution be taken up at once.

Although Cannon had the power to rule Norris out of order, he could not prevent an appeal against that ruling and hence a vote by the whole House. "Uncle Joe," noting that many Republican regulars were absent, realized the insurgent Republicans together with Democratic help might have enough votes to pass a motion for reversal. So, instead of announcing his ruling at once, he let debate open on the procedural issue while hasty summonses went

PRESERVING AMERICA'S NATURAL WEALTH

This map shows the location of the government projects in Theodore Roosevelt's far-reaching program of conservation and reclamation. In his seven and a half years as President, America was enriched with some 148 million acres of national forests, five national parks covering 213,886 acres, 1.4 million acres of national monuments, wildlife refuges occupying 434,293 acres, 1.5 million acres of land reclaimed by irrigation. The total area affected by all of Roosevelt's conservation projects amounted to more than 151 million acres—almost the size of the state of Texas.

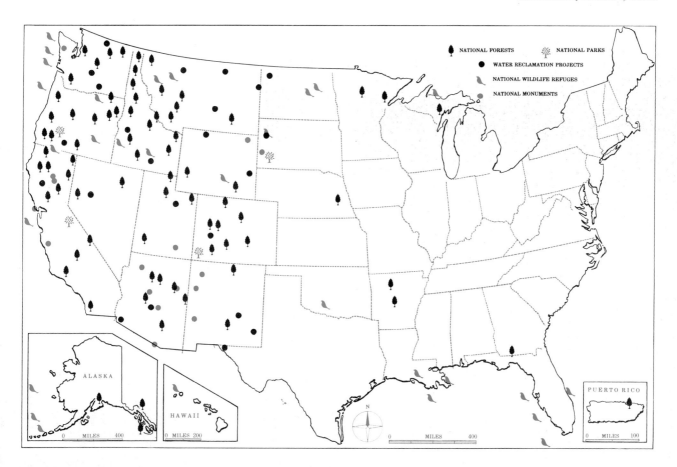

out to the absent regulars. His partisans on the floor conducted a virtual filibuster. For 26 hours the chamber remained in continuous session. Then, during a short recess, feverish negotiations went on in the cloakrooms.

When the House reconvened the next morning, most of the representatives were present, and the galleries were packed. The Speaker declared Norris' motion out of order. His ruling was appealed. In the votes that followed, the insurgents and Democrats joined forces and the Norris rules were adopted in essence. They stripped the Speaker of the power to assign members to committees, and they removed him from the powerful House Rules Committee.

Ashen-faced, Cannon declared that since the vote had proved that the Republicans were no longer in the majority, he would entertain a motion to replace him. But, partly from the sentimental wish to spare the proud old man another humiliation, partly from unwillingness to affiliate formally with the Democrats, the insurgents decided not to unseat him.

The autumn elections in 1910 gave the insurgents added strength. Many Republican candidates based their campaigns on opposition to the unpopular tariff and to the regular party leaders—Cannon, Aldrich and Taft. Although the conservatives and the Administration closed ranks to fight these upstarts, the progressive Republicans won conventions and primaries one after another. Forty-one incumbent regulars were defeated. In November more regulars lost to Democrats. In the new Congress the Democratic party had an absolute majority in the House, and Democrats and progressives together controlled the Senate.

Though bitterly at odds with the progressives, Taft did not stop pressing for reforms. With the votes of the insurgents and Democrats, he actually passed some bills and, in all, he amassed a record that included some notable progressive achievements. Among other things, he started twice as many antitrust suits in four years as Roosevelt had in seven. But Taft's reform accomplishments were ignored as the progressives scanned the field to find a new standard-bearer for the forthcoming presidential election.

Nebraska Representative George W. Norris, a progressive Republican, often angered conservative colleagues by following his conscience instead of regular party lines. But Speaker Joe Cannon, his power curtailed by Norris' resolution, paid him a sincere compliment: "If any member of your gang had to be elected, I'd rather it was you than any other. . . ."

FOR their 1912 candidate some progressives favored Senator Robert M. La Follette of Wisconsin. Most, however, wanted Roosevelt. The question was whether the ex-President would run.

After returning from his foreign travels, Roosevelt had discouraged all talk of his candidacy. But for him politics was an irresistible temptation. Although he kept aloof from the movement against Taft, he made speeches during the congressional campaign of 1910 that gave aid and slogans to candidates who were fighting the Administration. In a major address at Osawatomie, Kansas, he reiterated in stronger terms his earlier appeals for a more powerful federal government to offset big business and to enforce better conditions for labor. This he labeled the "New Nationalism."

Taft, meanwhile, took great pains to avoid trouble with Roosevelt. In the autumn of 1911, however, he authorized his Attorney General to file an antitrust suit against United States Steel. When the briefs were published the President discovered to his dismay that he had unintentionally challenged Roosevelt to open warfare.

The issue harked back to the Panic of 1907, when Roosevelt had helped stabilize the economy by aiding financier J. P. Morgan. This aid included permission for U.S. Steel to acquire control of the Tennessee Coal and Iron

Company. When asked if the transaction would be an antitrust violation, Roosevelt had assured Morgan that he would not so treat it. Afterward the criticism persisted that U.S. Steel had been granted an unfair advantage over competitors, and Roosevelt was repeatedly accused of having sacrificed the public interest. No charge angered him more. It was the same Tennessee Coal and Iron purchase that formed the basis for the Justice Department suit; and Roosevelt, confronted with briefs that made it appear he had been duped by Morgan, concluded that Taft intended to attack him personally.

Roosevelt retaliated with a free-swinging denunciation of Taft. At once the campaign for his nomination, which had lagged for want of encouragement, sprang to life. Moreover it now had fresh support. A number of Republican regulars, despairing of a Taft victory, showed a readiness to turn to Roosevelt as the only man strong enough to carry in candidates for lesser offices. Some men in big business, vexed by Taft's dogged pursuit of trusts, showed an awareness that they might be more comfortable under Roosevelt's New Nationalism. By early 1912 there was a roaring boom for Roosevelt's nomination.

Roosevelt played his cards shrewdly. He waited for enough support from the regulars to give him a fighting chance at victory, and enough popular demand for him to drown out any accusations of personal ambition. On February 21, 1912, with his conditions met, he declared, "My hat is in the ring."

But the very day that Roosevelt announced his candidacy, he virtually crippled his chances for success. In Columbus, Ohio, the ex-President said that conservative courts should not be able to frustrate progressive legislatures. He advocated referendum and recall procedures, by which voters could reverse judicial decisions.

This heresy against the traditional system of checks and balances was too much for most men of conservative leanings. Businessmen, newspaper editors and politicians erupted in criticism of Roosevelt. Nonetheless, the ex-President's popular appeal continued undiminished. In nearly all the states which held direct presidential primaries, he swamped his rival. But, with few exceptions, organization Republicans and businessmen turned away. One by one, old friends from the House and Senate told Roosevelt sadly that they could not side with him.

At the same time, Taft met adversity with a new and unsuspected vigor. He threw all of his resources into the contest for convention delegates. Local organizations were told to back Taft or lose all federal patronage. Hurt and angered by a stream of personal abuse from Roosevelt, Taft replied in kind. In April he cried out in a bitter speech: "Condemn me if you will, but condemn me by other witnesses than Theodore Roosevelt. I was a man of straw; but I have been a man of straw long enough. Every man who has blood in his body, and who has been misrepresented as I have . . . is forced to fight."

By June, when the national convention met in Chicago, the Taft forces were in control. Dominating the Committee on Credentials, they denied most of the claims of Roosevelt delegations and seated men who would do the Administration's bidding. Tempers flared. To Mr. Dooley's readers, the struggle was just about what he had predicted: "a combynation iv th' Chicago fire, Saint Bartholomew's massacree, the battle iv th' Boyne, th' life iv Jesse James, an' th' night iv th' big wind."

Rhode Island Senator Nelson W. Aldrich, champion of big business and the high tariff, wielded such power that he was dubbed "boss of the Senate," both as a compliment and as a criticism. His admirers went further, calling him "manager of the United States," and one actually claimed that he came "nearer to filling that rôle than even the President himself."

Frustrated, Roosevelt made a fateful decision. He would walk out of the convention and create his own party. He realized that the split in Republican ranks would probably mean his own defeat as well as Taft's but he was determined to take revenge on Taft and the regulars. He denounced the proceedings as fraudulent. His backers called another convention to meet in the same city and choose a Progressive candidate.

Several hundred responded. Among them were a handful of rich businessmen who sympathized with the New Nationalism and the few machine politicians who had broken with the regular party. But the great majority were high-minded amateurs—muckrakers, social workers, sponsors of movements for the initiative and referendum, toilers in local good-government campaigns. Their convention took on the air of crusade, and campaign songs rang out to the tunes of hymns. Roosevelt epitomized the mood when he said, "Our cause is based on the eternal principle of righteousness. . . ."

Roosevelt, of course, became the nominee, with Hiram Johnson of California as his running mate. The platform, supplemented by an eloquent speech, which Roosevelt labeled his "Confession of Faith," contained the period's fullest and most vigorous declaration of progressive principles.

It declared that government should be made more responsive to the public will. Toward this end it advocated direct primaries, initiative and referendum laws, recall of judicial decisions, easier procedures for amending the federal Constitution, and wider suffrage, including votes for women.

It urged action by the federal government to curb the powers and privileges of large economic interests. Its specific proposals included broader conservation programs, regulation of interstate industries and supervision of stock and bond trading.

The platform also called for legislation in behalf of the underprivileged—federal laws fixing minimum wages and maximum hours, abolishing child labor, setting up unemployment compensation and old-age pensions.

The Progressive party had little in the way of state and local political machinery except what it improvised or captured from regular Republican organizations. Its popular label, the Bull Moose party, told the story of what it was. Roosevelt was the Bull Moose; it was his party and it would last beyond the 1912 campaign only if he kept it alive. But what it stood for, and what he said for it, transcended this single contest for the presidency. Its promises summed up progressivism's answers to the challenges created by an age of industrialization.

DELEGATES to the Democratic nominating convention in Baltimore knew that the candidate whom they chose would almost certainly be elected President. William Jennings Bryan had supporters. So did other battle-scarred exponents of the farmer-centered reform philosophy. So did conservatives in the Grover Cleveland tradition. And so did one Democrat who was a progressive—Governor Woodrow Wilson of New Jersey.

Only 10 years earlier Wilson had been a professor of political economy at Princeton, known chiefly as the author of some provocative works on government and American history. The trustees of his university had noticed his administrative talents and in 1902 appointed him president of Princeton. In that job he not only proved his executive abilities but also showed a strain of stubborn determination and a capacity to lead and to inspire.

Early autos like the 1909 Reo and 1914 Nationals (above) were the center of a peculiar controversy. Many people worried about the sex of the new cars—were they "he" or "she"? The French, traditionally the best judges of such things, said "he." But Americans disagreed. An early Reo advertisement declared, "She is a Pleasure Car . . . for all who ride in her."

In 1910, when the New Jersey Democratic machine found itself endangered by a reform upsurge, the bosses thought of Wilson as a gubernatorial candidate. They asked him to run and succeeded in electing him. But they were totally unable to control his actions as governor. To their dismay he demonstrated a powerful grasp of legislative politics, and overcoming old-guard opposition from both parties, he forced passage of one reform bill after another. These established a direct primary, penalties for corrupt corporative practices, greater protection for workmen, controls to regulate railroads and public utilities. In two short years Wilson established a reputation as one of the most effective of progressive governors.

Actually, there was a basic difference between Wilson's political philosophy and Roosevelt's. As the alternative to the New Nationalism, Wilson advocated a "New Freedom." In his view the federal government should legislate the restoration of free competition among relatively small economic units and then confine itself to enforcing obedience. Although he had sponsored welfare bills, he regarded these as state, not federal, matters. He did not favor, as Roosevelt did, adding greatly to the powers or functions of the federal government.

Partly because he combined these Jeffersonian views with a fine progressive record, Wilson was more than acceptable to a number of regulars at the Democratic convention in Baltimore. Partly because he was born in Virginia and brought up in Georgia, he was second choice for Southerners who arrived as backers of Alabama congressman Oscar W. Underwood. After prolonged balloting the contest narrowed to Wilson and Champ Clark of Missouri, Cannon's successor as Speaker of the House. On the 46th ballot the Southerners threw their votes to the New Jerseyite and Wilson became the nominee.

THUS the nation faced a choice among Roosevelt, the militant progressive; Wilson, the moderate progressive; Taft, the ex-progressive; and Eugene V. Debs, the Socialist. Wilson had a freshness of appeal that his rivals could not match. He did not represent the lost cause of farmer domination. He came from an urbanized, industrialized state, and as governor he had successfully grappled with the new problems arising from the mushrooming growth of cities and the concentration of capital. His program was less radical than Roosevelt's, and it did not alienate moderates as did T.R.'s.

In the November balloting, 6,296,547 voted for Wilson, 4,188,571 for Roosevelt and 3,486,720 for Taft, while Debs received 900,672 votes. Although Wilson was elected President with only a plurality of the popular vote, there could be no doubt whatever that the people had spoken out for reform—and for a new brand of progressive leadership.

The new President was in an enviable position. His party had workable majorities in both houses and, if there were conservatives among the Democrats, there were plenty of progressive Republicans to offset them. Moreover, the elections of 1912 had brought such a heavy Democratic turnover that almost 40 per cent of their bloc were newcomers, too inexperienced to have formed rigid opinions. Perhaps more important, the congressional freshmen needed all the federal patronage they could get, so they were eager to earn good marks in the President's book. For all these reasons, there was a greater opportunity for presidential leadership than at almost any time in the past.

Wilson skillfully exploited this situation. He abandoned the presidential custom, followed since Jefferson's time, of sending messages to Congress to be

Despite cries of "disgusting and indecent," "animal dances" like the turkey trot (top) and the grizzly bear (bottom) swept the country in the second decade of the century. A New Jersey town jailed a young lady for 50 days for doing the turkey trot. And in Philadelphia 15 girls were fired when their employer found them turkey-trotting on their lunch hour.

read aloud by a clerk. Instead he addressed Congress himself. He wished to demonstrate, he said, "that the President of the United States is a person, not a mere department of the Government hailing Congress from some isolated island of jealous power . . . that he is a human being trying to cooperate with other human beings in a common service."

In countless conferences with the legislators, Wilson reasoned patiently about points of difference, invited suggestions for improvements or changes, applauded men who stood with him and sometimes, ever so politely, warned of dire consequences for those who defied him. As he pursued these tactics, Wilson provoked a wide range of reactions. Thin and long-faced, with a mouth set in a hard, disapproving line, he looked out from behind rimless spectacles with an air of stern concentration. Men who had dealt with him only a few times found him forbidding. After several interviews some still thought him cold, reserved, impersonal. Most who came to know him well discovered that a gay smile could transform his face and that he possessed a warmth that went far beyond his old-fashioned courtliness. Some congressmen became devoted to him; others feared him; many were overawed by the power of his mind and the nobility of his public utterances. The reasons why they followed him were varied, but they did follow.

A 1913 cartoon shows "The People" paddling through smooth water after the rough passage of the 16th Amendment. The first personal income tax that was collected affected so restricted a group of Americans that humorist George Fitch optimistically declared, "It will be an exclusive circle, this income-tax class—one which the ordinary . . . man cannot hope to enter."

As President, Wilson had three major objectives: to revise the tariff, to reform the banking system and to write a new antitrust law. In putting tariff reform at the top of his legislative agenda, Wilson was not making the tactical error that Taft had made. Some Democrats were protectionists. But his party was traditionally opposed to high duties, advocating a tariff for revenue only, and a number of Democratic congressmen had been elected in 1910 and 1912 on the basis of their opposition to the Taft Administration's tariff act. For Wilson, the tariff was the safest and simplest starting point for the three battles he intended to wage.

Democrats in the House prepared a bill that would greatly reduce protective duties on manufactured items but retain or add to the imposts on agricultural products, raw wool and leather boots and shoes. Wilson opposed all exceptions and demanded a law abolishing "everything that bears even the semblance of privilege or of any kind of artificial advantage."

He succeeded in getting the bill rewritten and passed by the House, but the Senate seemed likely to restore some protective duties. Then Wilson declared that lobbyists for special interests were swarming around members of that body. "It is of serious interest to the country that the people at large should have no lobby and be voiceless in these matters," he declared, "while great bodies of astute men seek to create an artificial opinion and to overcome the interests of the public for their private profit."

This announcement created a sensation. Senators of both parties denied that it was true. Republican leaders goaded the Senate into setting up a committee to investigate the charge, expecting a report that would cost the President his credit with the public and damage his influence on Capitol Hill.

The reverse happened. The committee was deluged with evidence of special-interest lobbying. Public disclosure was made of stocks owned by certain senators, indicating that some profited from the protective duties they had voted. The Democratic majority hastened to get the tariff bill out of committee and finally passed it in much the form that the President had requested.

This Underwood Tariff Act represented a resounding triumph for Wilson. Protectionism had survived every onslaught since the Civil War, but in a few months Wilson had dealt it a great defeat.

The substance of his victory, however, proved less important than its symbolism, for the outbreak of war in Europe denied the new system a practical test. In retrospect, the part of the 1913 statute that seems most noteworthy is one that had been secondary in Wilson's mind. It was the provision, authorized by a new constitutional amendment, for putting a minuscule tax on personal incomes. Even more significant was the strong personal role Wilson had played in putting the bill through.

While the tariff law was still under debate, Wilson launched his second major effort. He asked Congress for far-reaching legislation to correct the flaws in the banking system that had been exposed in the Panic of 1907. The main weakness was the lack of any reliable method to regulate the supply of money. Banks had to keep on hand whatever seemed necessary to meet withdrawals. In good times they had a cash excess in their vaults, yet in bad times they were often hard pressed to meet demands. Wilson wanted to provide a more elastic currency that would fluctuate with the amount of credit required by the economy. He believed this could best be done by setting up a system of central banks in various parts of the country, which could hold the reserve funds of existing commercial banks and make them available to accommodate business needs.

The President entered long and intricate negotiations with financiers and politicians. While most bankers approved of reorganizing the banking system, they stood firm for private control of any central banks. But many Democrats and progressives argued for government control over banking in order to break the monopoly on credit that they believed New York bankers possessed. After weighing all the evidence, Wilson insisted that while the regional banks should be privately owned and operated, they must be controlled and coordinated by a Federal Reserve Board appointed by the government. This program, incorporated in the Federal Reserve Act, also made the government solely responsible for the issuance of currency.

MANY conservatives were displeased by the bill, charging that the President meant to socialize banking. On the other hand some Bryanites and progressives demanded more radical reform, claiming that the bill would merely legalize the money trust and place it under government protection. In addition to publicly controlled regional banks, they wanted the law to destroy the power wielded by private bankers through interlocking directorates. Moreover, they wanted the system to grant short-term agricultural credits. Threatened with a revolt by agrarian members of his own party, Wilson made some concessions to satisfy them. Bryan, whom Wilson had appointed Secretary of State, finally swung the disgruntled representatives of the farmers around to supporting the President. Then the amended bill met fierce opposition from a large part of the banking community. But Wilson held his ground. After six months of hearings and debate in Congress, the Federal Reserve Act finally passed in December 1913. Though considerably different from the measure the President had originally wanted, the act was not substantially different from the bill Wilson had proposed to Congress. For him it was a triumph that matched in significance the Underwood Tariff.

Progressives in the 1913 Congress were so strong that they could turn a bill intended to increase private control over reserve banks into a victory for federal control. President Wilson demanded public currency control "so that the banks may be the instruments, not the masters" of the economy. The cartoon shows Wilson "reading the death warrant" of big money trusts.

A new antitrust law was supposed to put the capstone on the Administration labors. A few weeks after the banking bill became law, Wilson began to press for passage of an act that would outlaw interlocking directorates, enumerate unfair trade practices and punish offenses against antitrust laws as criminal acts. Approved by enemies of big business, this bill promised to curtail big business and high finance and to improve the lot of small farmers and small-business men. In a rush of enthusiasm the House passed it by a vote of 275 to 54.

Charles Evans Hughes addresses a county fair in New York during his successful campaign for governor in 1908. Hughes's rich beard was the subject of many jokes, not all of them kind. Even Teddy Roosevelt, stumping for Hughes, could not resist commenting on it. T.R. said that the only difference between progressive Wilson and progressive Hughes was "a shave."

AFTER the bill's introduction, however, Wilson began to have second thoughts. While the loud protest from businessmen made little impression on him, he was impressed by the quiet counsel of some distinguished progressives. They asserted that it would be impossible to define and outlaw all unfair business practices, and they convinced Wilson that the most effective control would be a governmental agency powerful enough to deal with particular abuses as they arose. When the House bill went to the Senate, the President began to work unobtrusively for some important changes.

The Congress also had before it a subsidiary measure that added slightly to the powers of Roosevelt's Bureau of Corporations and renamed it the Interstate Trade Commission. Wilson decided to recommend that the senators concentrate on this bill rather than on the antitrust act. He suggested that Congress, instead of specifying crimes against competition and affixing penalties, might give the Trade Commission authority to conduct investigations and to order an offending firm to cease any unfair trade practices. Despite the protests of some conservatives, the Senate modified both bills as Wilson desired and the House concurred. The final antitrust law, the Clayton Act, simply strengthened some parts of the Sherman Act and declared that labor organizations should not be treated by the courts as conspiracies in restraint of trade. More significant was the new enactment called the Federal Trade Commission Act, which created a government agency with power to oversee and restrain practically all big business.

In shifting his emphasis from the Clayton Act to the Trade Commission Act, Wilson had clearly moved away from the principles of his own New Freedom, toward those of Roosevelt's New Nationalism. This change in his position caused some surprise, for Wilson usually spoke as if his positions were immutable. Actually he was a practical man as well as a theoretician; once he concluded that it was advisable to increase the role of government, he had no hesitation in adopting appropriate measures, even if an opponent had advanced them first. Wilson went even further; he openly declared his strong commitment to progressive ideals. It was not altogether by coincidence that Wilson's announcement came in 1916: by then it seemed certain that the Republican party would reunite and that he would be competing with its presidential nominee for the votes of erstwhile Progressives.

During the 1916 campaign Wilson presented Congress with a full new legislative program. Using the same tactics as in 1913 and 1914, he won from it a series of welfare acts—special credit facilities for farmers; a model workman's compensation law for federal employees; an emergency bill averting a railroad strike by decreeing an eight-hour day for railroad employees; and a statute barring the products of child labor from interstate commerce. Wilson also advocated an eight-hour day for all workers and endorsed business mergers for the purpose of competing in foreign markets. The President had become spokesman for all the varieties of progressivism.

The wide range of Wilson's progressive program created a difficult problem for his Republican opponent in the 1916 elections. Charles Evans Hughes had made his reputation in an investigation that exposed the financial misdeeds of large insurance companies. He had become a reform governor in New York, then a liberal Supreme Court justice. The pressure on him to leave the safe Court post and make the campaign had been based on his presumed appeal to the ex-Progressives. Hughes, as the owner of a distinguished record of reform and as the nominee of the majority party, had reason to think that his chances for victory were excellent.

As the campaign got under way, however, Hughes discovered that Wilson had pre-empted progressive causes and that the President's domestic record left the Republicans with no real issue. Hughes attacked Wilson at random, offering nothing constructive in return. As for foreign policy, Wilson and Hughes both said they would endeavor to keep the United States out of the European war. Here, however, Hughes was embarrassed by the support of Roosevelt, who belligerently called for a strong stand abroad. Hughes was further handicapped by continuing division within many state and local Republican organizations. Hughes's campaign quickly proved a disappointment. As early as August the New York *World* editorialized, "No other candidate for president within the memory of living man ever ran downhill so rapidly."

Yet Wilson in 1912 had been elected by just 42 per cent of the popular vote; and it was by no means certain that the strength of his Administration could overcome the normal Republican majority.

In fact, the 1916 election was one of the closest in United States history. Wilson went to bed convinced he had lost. But when the returns came in from the West Coast, California had gone Democratic and Wilson won a second term by a narrow margin. But that narrow margin was in itself a smashing victory; it represented a net gain by Wilson of nearly three million votes.

Citizen Hughes vainly attempts to warm his hands over the cold stove of California, the state that cost him the presidency. His defeat there, by 3,806 votes, was sealed by a sharp split in state Republican ranks. An astute observer noted that "a man of sense with a dollar" for drinks would have healed the rift, won Hughes the state—and thus the election.

CONTEMPORARY observers had some warrant for feeling that the 1916 election completed the triumph of progressivism. Of the two candidates, Wilson was the one who symbolized energetic, progressive government; and a substantial number of Progressive votes had helped return him to office. The principles espoused by progressives had gained widespread acceptance. In 1900 a great amount of power had rested in the hands of the very wealthy. By 1917 much of that power was subject to the challenge of officials who were responsible to the American public. J. P. Morgan was dead. His house had withdrawn from control of 30 banks and corporations. No mogul had taken his place or seemed able to.

Some Americans still held to the tradition that "that government governs best which governs least." But the national ideal of individualism had been strongly modified by the needs of the time. To meet the problems of vast industrial growth and a complex economy, government could scarcely avoid taking an increasing role in the nation's life. City, state and federal administrations were performing a host of new services—operating public utilities, enforcing tenement laws, regulating transportation charges, policing business competition, and even in some cases decreeing the hours of labor. The progressive movement had made government a counterweight to the plutocracy.

CRUSADERS for conservation, Theodore Roosevelt and old John Muir meet in Yosemite, California. In 1903 the two men camped there for four days; T.R. left convinced that "vigorous action must be taken" to save the nation's natural wealth and beauty.

The pioneer years of conservation

THE great westward expansion, during the second half of the 19th Century, had revealed to America the wealth of its resources. Settlers thought of that wealth as inexhaustible. It wasn't. Yearly a billion tons of soil was washed into the Gulf of Mexico. Flocks and droves of birds and animals were being reduced to extinction or near-extinction. Sixty million buffalo had roamed the plains, but by 1900 about a thousand remained. Billions of passenger pigeons had flown through the land. By 1915 none remained.

In 1901 Theodore Roosevelt became President. Appalled by the wastage of national wealth, he began a program of conservation and reclamation. In 1902 the Reclamation Act was passed; projects to make arid earth productive were begun in Nevada and Arizona. In 1903 the first Wildlife Refuge was established. Under the Antiquities Act of 1906, Roosevelt put regions of special scientific or historic interest under government protection. When Gifford Pinchot, his Chief Forester, declared that America's forests had been so reduced that "we have in store timber enough for only twenty or thirty years," T.R. set about saving timber. When he took office the nation had 47 million acres of national forests; when he left, 195 million acres. He doubled the number of national parks. It was his work that saved, for public pleasure and controlled harvesting, some of the nation's remaining natural heritage.

ROOSEVELT DAM remains a prototype for big reclamation projects. Completed in 1911, it provided 240,000 acres of land around Phoenix, Arizona, with irrigation water.

The nation's timberland saved for posterity

AMERICA'S vast forests had been greatly depleted by the time Theodore Roosevelt moved to protect them. Between 1860 and 1885, railroad and lumber companies had acquired 600,000 square miles of land, much of it richly forested. Their forestry policy was: cut and get out. Timberlands in the public domain were administered by the Land Office, a bureau that was mainly interested in getting rid of them. Responsibility for the forests was so divided that no constructive program could be developed. When Gifford Pinchot took over the impotent Forestry Division in 1898 he had a total staff of 10 and three pieces of outdoor equipment. Roosevelt promptly secured legislation that gave Pinchot power to conserve the woodlands; foresters were given forests to care for, and the nation added to its timberland reserves. Under Pinchot, trained men were assigned to prevent fire, control grazing, mining and lumbering within the forests, and make sure that fees were paid for private use of public lands. Federal forests were, at last, to be more effectively preserved and carefully used.

A TROPICAL PROFUSION, Caribbean National Forest sprawls high above the humid Puerto Rican coastal plain. Established by Roosevelt in 1903, it serves mainly as a research area.

A PATCHWORK OF EVERGREENS rises in an experimental area of Arapaho National Forest, Colorado (opposite), where 22,000 acres serve for study of forestry and watershed management.

A NETWORK OF LAKES stretches through Superior National Forest, Minnesota (above). The three-million-acre forest has some 600 square miles of untouched primitive wilderness.

"Nothing . . . more beautiful"

Half Dome Mountain (left) juts 4,850 feet above the valley floor, and two waterfalls, Vernal and Nevada (center and right), plunge a combined distance of 911 feet in Yosemite National Park, California. In 1864 Congress granted Yosemite Valley to California "for public use, resort, and recreation." But state

administration proved inadequate. Trees were felled in vast numbers, much of the valley was privately fenced off, sheep grazing went unchecked. Roosevelt was appalled by what he had seen at Yosemite. He returned to Washington eager to protect the park. "There is nothing in the world more beautiful than Yosemite . . . groves of giant Sequoias and redwoods," said T. R., ". . . and the people should see to it that they are preserved for their children and their children's children." In 1906 the valley, returned to the federal government, became the heart of what is now a 1,200-square-mile national park.

111

Devils Tower, in northeast Wyoming, rises 865 feet from its base. The first national monument, it was set apart as a historic site in 1906.

PHANTOM SHIP, a tree-covered island, rises out of Oregon's Crater Lake. Formed millennia ago when a volcano exploded and collapsed, the lake became a national park in 1902.

Saving the evidence of the continent's past

THE Antiquities Act of 1906 empowered the President to preserve landmarks, structures and objects of historic or scientific interest as national monuments. Within three years, Roosevelt set aside 18 such areas. Swift action was necessary. In Arizona's Petrified Forest *(right)* souvenir hunters and gem collectors were hacking and blasting the stone logs for the amethyst crystals found within them. A mill had been set up to pound the logs into abrasives. Crater Lake *(above)* was at that time so remote that it seemed safe, but conservationists realized that it, too, needed protection. Bypassing a Congress reluctant to conserve wilderness, Roosevelt applied the Antiquities Act generously. When Congress refused to create more national parks, Roosevelt created them by edict, simply by calling them national monuments. In this way Grand Canyon, for example, was set aside in 1908 and thus rescued from commercial exploitation.

PETRIFIED PINES, once buried in mud and sand of ancient seas, lie in northern Arizona. Made a national monument in 1906, Petrified Forest is now a national park.

An architectural heritage rescued from ruin

AS a young man Theodore Roosevelt had written a fine history of the American westward movement; as President he welcomed the powers given him by the Antiquities Act to protect the remnants of the peoples who had placed their mark on the land.

It was none too soon to begin the work of preserving the ruins of the cliff dwellings of Mesa Verde *(below)*, which were built by successive Indian civilizations between the First and the 14th Centuries. These ancient buildings were rapidly becoming a hunting ground for commercial exploiters who vandalized the caves and sold their loot to tourists. In 1906 the Mesa Verde plateau became a national park; it remains the only park set aside primarily for its history of human habitation.

The Spanish mission churches are far more recent than the Mesa Verde ruins, but many of them had been abandoned and vandals considered them fair game. The graceful church at Tumacacori *(right)* had been stripped almost bare before Roosevelt preserved it for future generations by designating it a national monument.

ANCIENT HOMES of pre-Columbian Indians, built of large, loaf-like stone blocks chipped to shape, stand beneath the protective overhang of rock in a canyon in Mesa Verde National Park.

A MISSION CHURCH *(right)*, completed in 1822, stands as a reminder of Spanish influence in southern Arizona. The first priest came to the region in 1691 and a church was built by 1698.

Protection for "all harmless wild things"

IN 1899 Theodore Roosevelt, then governor of New York, wrote: "I would like to see all harmless wild things, but especially all birds, protected. . . . When I hear of the destruction of a species I feel just as if all the works of some great writer had perished." As President, Roosevelt set out to protect as many "harmless wild things" as he could. His efforts came after years of destructive waste. During the 1880s more than five million birds had been killed annually to make hats for women. (One bird-and-hat-watcher, walking through Manhattan, counted 20 species of dead birds on women's heads.) Railroads had attracted customers by advertising buffalo shoots from train windows. In most states, hunters gunned for long seasons and without limit. In Louisiana,

one hunter killed 430 ducks in a day; another, in North Dakota, came back after four hours' shooting with 700 pounds of wildfowl. Two horses pulled in that load, and the hunter kept on shooting for a month. In America, five species of mammals and 15 species and subspecies of birds have been utterly destroyed, another 24 species of mammals and 33 species of birds brought close to extinction. President Roosevelt, anxious to save what was left, set aside many refuges. The first, founded in 1903, was at Pelican Island in Florida, a nesting place for pelicans, herons and the white ibis. Before leaving office, the energetic conservationist established 51 bird reservations and four big-game refuges. A remnant of the continent's originally abundant wildlife was rescued.

Canada geese, wintering in the U.S., float on a protected pond. This large, wide-ranging wildfowl, shot without limit until 1913 when the

AN OLYMPIC ELK, his antlers in "velvet," rests after grazing. Once common, by 1900 these elk were reduced to a small herd, concentrated near Mt. Olympus, Washington. Roosevelt preserved the area and helped save the species.

LAZY WALRUSES bask off the Alaska coast. Alaskan wildlife refuges were established in 1909 but the walrus remained unprotected until 1956.

first federal law regulating hunting of migratory birds was passed, was made the emblem of the nation's Fish and Wildlife Refuge program.

6. THE
BIG STICK

WHILE progressives and conservatives were struggling for supremacy at home during the early years of the 20th Century, an equally significant debate was taking place over the role the United States should play in world affairs. By 1850 America's growth in population, industrial production and military potential had made it a match for some of the great European powers. By 1890 it had surpassed nearly all of them. But most Americans still thought that their country's promised time of supremacy was far in the future. More important, perhaps, was the fact that European nations still looked down on the United States and treated it as a second-rate power whose actions and policies could have little effect on their own.

The "splendid little war" of 1898 made America a great power. Americans soon realized that they could compete on equal terms with established powers like Britain, France, Germany, Austria-Hungary and Russia. European statesmen realized with equal alacrity that the United States had become one of the forces that could shape the political destinies of the planet.

The Old World responded by exploring the possibility of drawing the United States into one alliance system or another. In Berlin there was talk of possible agreement for German-American co-operation against Britain; London analyzed formulas for ending long-standing issues with the United States and creating a tacit alliance between England and America. When the German kaiser and the czar of Russia held a conference in 1903, the kaiser noted

CLEAVING THE ISTHMUS, an army of workmen attacks the stupendous construction task in Panama. Artist Jonas Lie entitled this painting *The Conquerors, Culebra Cut.*

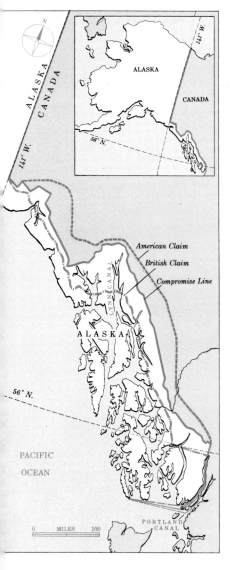

THE ALASKAN BOUNDARY
SETTLEMENT OF 1903

*In 1825 a treaty between Russia
and Britain loosely defined the
southern boundary of Alaska as
running inland to the Portland
Canal, then up the canal until it
reached a range of mountains. It
then ran north, not more than 30
miles from the coast, until it connected with the 141st Meridian.
But when gold was discovered, the
British disputed the line and asserted control of the Lynn Canal,
which was the shorter route to
the gold fields. In 1903 a commission of two Canadians, three Americans and a pro-U.S. Briton drew
up a compromise favoring the U.S.*

that the United States disturbed him even more than did England; the czar
"observed that America alarms him too."

In the United States, debate over alternative future policies was loud and
confused. Many people—like William Jennings Bryan, Grover Cleveland and
spokesmen for the Boston-centered Anti-Imperialist League—held that the
nation should hew to its old course: concentrate on bettering itself at home,
avoid any involvement in the politics of either Europe or Asia, run no risk
of war, reduce spending on the Army and Navy. These ideas received considerable support, for as always, there was a powerful current of isolationism
in the country.

There were opposing voices strongly urging bold and adventurous policies. Albert J. Beveridge, a young lawyer from Indiana, had been designated
United States senator in 1899 as a champion of imperialism. Brooks Adams,
the dour, brilliant, painfully shy historian, wrote in 1900 that the United
States should contemplate the possibility of military struggle to secure world
supremacy. Naval strategist Alfred Thayer Mahan proposed that America
should make itself the dominant force in Asia, cut a canal through Central
America so that the Caribbean could replace the Mediterranean as the principal route for European-Asiatic commerce, ring the Caribbean with American naval bases and make that sea as indubitably an American preserve as
in ancient times the Mediterranean was Roman.

Thus the issue was drawn. One group wanted America to save its strength
for domestic problems and let happen what would abroad. The other argued
with equal vehemence that America should thrust itself outward, seize such
advantages as it could and attempt to establish dominance or at least pre-
eminence throughout the world.

THE men in Washington who had to make decisions sought some middle
way between these two extremes. McKinley never committed himself wholly to either position, although he leaned toward the activists. For
China he invoked the vague principle of the Open Door in 1899: Through Secretary of State John Hay he told the major powers, in effect, that while the
existence of spheres of interest in China was a fact, there should be no bar-
riers to trade in these areas. In 1900, when European powers and Japan
combined with America to suppress the Boxer Uprising against foreigners in
China, the United States said that it wanted China to retain its territorial
integrity. But McKinley carefully refrained from any commitment to go to
war to protect the Open Door or defend Chinese independence.

In the Western Hemisphere the McKinley Administration—strongly influenced by the emphatic views of Mahan and other imperialists—was able to
go somewhat further in the direction of the expansionists. McKinley endorsed
the Central American canal project. In addition he concluded a treaty with
Denmark for the purchase of the Danish West Indies (or Virgin Islands), one
of the sites indispensable for naval control of the Caribbean, according to
Mahan. (Though ratified by the Senate, the treaty was defeated in the Danish Rigsdag, and the islands did not become America's till 1917.) But even
in the Caribbean, McKinley's acceptance of the Beveridge-Mahan policy was
hesitant and cautious.

It was in Europe that McKinley's policies were most daring, and this was
almost certainly due to Hay. The Secretary of State had been ambassador to

Britain in the late 1890s, when the potential importance of Anglo-American friendship had dawned most brightly on English statesmen and journalists, and he came back firmly convinced that English and American interests complemented each other.

Hay agreed with English statesmen that the first step toward an entente had to be the removal of needless irritants. One was the unsettled question of the boundary between southeastern Alaska and western Canada. Under varying interpretations of old agreements, both the United States and Canada claimed the mouths of all rivers that drained the gold-rich Klondike. To calm the passions that had risen over this issue, Hay arranged a temporary settlement.

Another irritant was the Clayton-Bulwer Treaty of 1850. Drawn up at a time when British interest and influence in Central America was possibly greater than that of the United States, the pact provided that neither of the two nations should build or operate an interoceanic canal except in partnership with the other. Now, however, Congress obviously had no intention either of sharing the work with Britain or of letting the English have any say in the canal's management. Under Hay's direction a new agreement was drawn giving the United States the right to build and operate a canal by itself, provided only that—as had been established with the Suez Canal—it remain open to the ships of all nations, although fortification was tacitly permitted to preserve the canal from destruction.

In the short time between the Spanish War and the death of McKinley, the government did not find a perfect middle way between what could loosely be called isolationism and activism, but the first steps were taken toward a definite break with the isolationist tradition.

Then suddenly, Theodore Roosevelt was President. Since he had been one of the first Americans to applaud Mahan's writing, it would have been reasonable to predict that his foreign policy would involve America even more in world politics. But this was not to be so. Although Roosevelt was sometimes to be bellicose (ignoring his own motto, "Speak softly and carry a big stick"), and was to cut something of a figure on the world stage, his Administration was to see America turn away from international involvement.

Although Roosevelt kept Hay as Secretary of State, he relied on him much less than had McKinley. In most instances Roosevelt was his own Secretary of State. Hay's personal policy of promoting a closer relationship with Britain went by the boards. While several of Roosevelt's close friends were Englishmen, he did not regard the English with any particular warmth. Certainly Roosevelt did not believe that there was any necessary identity between British and American national objectives, as was soon shown by the Alaskan boundary dispute.

Hay's temporary settlement was showing signs of strain. After Roosevelt took office, Hay, acting for the President, arranged that a six-man commission, consisting of three Americans, two Canadians and an Englishman, should adjudicate the boundary dispute. But Roosevelt let it be known to the British government that if the commission ruled against the United States, he would send troops into the disputed zone, occupy it and draw his own boundary. Despite this provocation, the British turned the other cheek. Their commissioner, Lord Alverstone, voted with the Americans on the key

Rear Admiral Alfred T. Mahan, whose theories on naval power greatly influenced U.S. foreign policy, nearly ended his career before it began. As a midshipman in 1859 Mahan asked to be assigned to the sloop-of-war "Levant." Fortunately his request was denied, and he went to another ship. The "Levant" sailed for the Pacific, was never heard of again.

issues, and the dispute was settled in 1903; the past irritant was removed. It could not, however, be said that the United States had shown any desire for better understanding or closer relations with Britain. All that was clear thus far was that Roosevelt intended to go it alone.

The first two years of Roosevelt's Administration also saw dramatic new developments in Western Hemisphere affairs. First came the Venezuelan crisis of 1902-1903. For some time the dictator of Venezuela, Cipriano Castro, had failed to pay off Venezuela's debts to European creditors. When European nationals were mistreated, he apologized perfunctorily if at all. By the fall of 1902 the British and Germans, followed by the Italians, agreed to apply pressure, first by presenting demands and then, if necessary, by using force against Castro. Before doing so, the countries asked Washington whether the United States would object. Since Castro had also behaved irresponsibly toward Americans, and since there were many earlier cases in which European powers had taken punitive action against Latin American states, Roosevelt gave his approval.

The demands were presented; Castro sneered; the European governments acted. British and German ships took station off the Venezuelan coast in December 1902. They seized Venezuelan gunboats, sank others, bombarded Puerto Cabello and declared a formal blockade.

S IMILAR activity in the past had gone practically unnoticed. Now American newspapers erupted with banner headlines and editorials that screamed that European powers were totally disregarding the Monroe Doctrine. It was almost a repeat performance of the kind of mass hysteria that America had witnessed before the 1898 intervention in Cuba.

When Castro capitulated, Roosevelt suggested an end to the blockade and the submission of the dispute to arbitration. Alerted to the seriousness of the situation by dispatches from their ambassadors in Washington, the three powers welcomed this solution.

Not long afterward, Roosevelt began to tell friends that he had sent the German kaiser an ultimatum, warning that if the German warships did not join the British in withdrawing, he would order the American battle fleet into action against them. By piecing together circumstantial evidence, some scholars have concluded that a mild warning of some kind may actually have been conveyed to Berlin. In neither the American nor the German archives, however, has any documentary proof of an ultimatum turned up.

An earlier incident in T. R.'s life throws some light on this peculiar episode. When at Harvard he competed for but never won the college lightweight boxing championship. Later, however, he wrote that he had been "lightweight champion at one time." One biographer, Henry Pringle, has charitably remarked: "He had wanted very much to be boxing champion, and with the years it seemed impossible to him that he had not really achieved that eminence." The same thing may have been true in the Venezuelan case. In retrospect Roosevelt may have felt that he should have sent the kaiser an ultimatum, and therefore it seemed impossible that he had not done so.

As the Venezuelan episode developed, Roosevelt began to realize that public opinion had completely accepted the idea that the United States was now the controlling power in the Western Hemisphere. If not at this moment, then fairly soon thereafter Roosevelt seems to have concluded that he needed to

Ferdinand de Lesseps was widely acclaimed as "The Great Frenchman" after he built the Suez Canal. He was an energetic 74 when he tackled the Panama Canal in 1880. Nine tragic years later, after accidents and disease in Panama had claimed the lives of 5,527 workers, he quit the bankrupt project with a broken spirit and a new name: "The Great Undertaker."

pursue a more energetic policy in the Caribbean if he were to keep in step with public opinion. At any rate, that inference can be drawn from the next consequential development: the case of Panama.

In June 1902 Congress had at last decided in favor of Panama as the site for an interoceanic canal. But the fight between the champions of Panama and of Nicaragua had been ferocious. The final bill provided that if the government failed to get rights in Panama within a reasonable time it should turn to Nicaragua. Congress also voted to buy up the French concession, under which Ferdinand de Lesseps had originally failed in his effort to dig a Panama canal.

Panama was then a department of the Republic of Colombia. The Colombian chargé d'affaires in Washington, under pressure exerted by Roosevelt and Hay, reluctantly agreed to a treaty that satisfied American demands. But Colombia's president, José M. Marroquín, had not approved his emissary's actions and now demanded more. Neither Roosevelt nor Hay would bend; they felt the Senate would probably not ratify the treaty if more generous terms were given Colombia. They held their ground, and in January 1903 the United States signed a treaty, renewable in perpetuity, granting it control of a six-mile-wide strip and promising Colombia $10 million outright and, after a period of years, an annual payment of $250,000.

Intense opposition to the treaty developed in Colombia, and on August 12, 1903, the Colombian senate voted unanimously to reject it. Roosevelt blurted out that the Colombians should be treated as "inefficient bandits." But because he was convinced that the Panama route was superior, he was unwilling to turn to Nicaragua. Moreover, he realized that the Nicaraguans, heartened by Colombian resistance, would probably make stiff and perhaps unacceptable demands. Yet Roosevelt could not simply drop the project. He genuinely believed that the canal would be "of well-nigh incalculable possibilities for the good of this country and the nations of mankind." Finally, he feared that abandonment of the canal would hurt his chances for re-election.

One path remained. Panama, cut off by jungles and highlands from all communication with Colombia except by sea, was in effect a Colombian colony. It had a long history of unsuccessful uprisings for independence from Colombia. In large measure Colombia's success in putting down the revolts reflected the aid given by the United States, which had a strong interest in protecting the American-owned Panama railroad. By treaty dating back to 1846, America had the right to intervene on its own initiative in order to preserve uninterrupted transit across the isthmus. Now that Colombia and the United States were at odds, there seemed a good chance that the Panamanians would make a new try for independence. If they did, the United States could take the position that any Colombian repression would interfere with transit, and invoking the 1846 treaty, it could use warships to stop Colombian troops from landing.

Senator Albert Beveridge embodied the duality of the expansionist era: He was a Progressive at home; abroad he was an uncompromising imperialist. In his first speech in the Senate, he said: "The Philippines are ours forever. . . . We will not renounce our part in the mission of our race ... [Give thanks] to Almighty God that He has marked us as His chosen people."

THERE remained the question of whether there would be a Panamanian revolution. Roosevelt was urged to take steps to bring one about, but he piously replied that, whatever other governments might do, the United States could not foment an insurrection. If, however, the President had not become convinced that the Panamanians would revolt sometime in 1903, perhaps he would have gone a little further in encouraging them.

On November 3, 1903, the revolution broke out. A Colombian contingent landed at Colón on the Caribbean side of the isthmus, but when American

Marines came ashore supported by the guns of the *Nashville*, the Colombian troops struck their tents and sailed for home. Panama City, on the Pacific side, was bombarded briefly by a Colombian gunboat. The revolt was almost bloodless; one man and one donkey were killed. Colombia could do nothing but protest. The United States recognized Panama's independence in a matter of days, and in a short time Panama signed a treaty containing nearly the same terms that Colombia had refused to ratify.

Americans mixed applause and criticism for the revolt and for Roosevelt's share in it. Roosevelt himself was later to boast about what he had done when he proclaimed in 1911, "I took the Canal Zone," thus playing into the hands of critics who interpreted his action in just such light. (In a belated and somewhat shamefaced gesture of apology, Congress in 1921 was to appropriate $25 million in reparations to Colombia.)

R OOSEVELT was extremely sensitive to popular feeling. From the mixed response to his action in Panama, he may have surmised that a goodly number of Americans expected their government to adhere to strict ethical standards. Or he may have felt merely that the public mood had changed— that the taste for energetic diplomacy, evident in the Venezuelan affair, had begun to wear off. Other events occurring at roughly the same time as Panama also affected him.

The entire international political situation was changing. In February 1904 the Japanese launched a surprise attack on the Russian fleet at Port Arthur (a maneuver to be repeated with equal success at Pearl Harbor in 1941) and started a war that promised to transform the Asian balance of power. In Europe, meanwhile, the British and French drew together in the Entente Cordiale. With France and Russia already allied, the shape of Europe's future could be discerned: two hostile blocs, the Anglo-French-Russian on one side and a German-Austro-Hungarian on the other, that menaced the peace of the world. Great power rivalries were more intense, and the potential risks to the United States, if it became entangled in these rivalries, were much greater. These facts unquestionably impressed themselves on Roosevelt, but beyond this it is difficult to say what motivated his next moves.

Roosevelt wrote voluminously about what he had done. Few other Presidents have put on paper so much about their years in office. But he was remarkably successful in keeping his inmost thoughts to himself. No one can make more than educated guesses about the reasons for his choices and decisions. But whether the causes lay in the specific domestic reaction to his Panama policy, in the general world situation, in larger considerations of domestic politics and policy, or in something altogether different, the fact remains that at some point between the autumn of 1903 and the spring of 1904, Roosevelt began to back away from adventurousness in foreign policy.

The retreat was not sudden. A nation, like a great ship, continues to move ahead long after its propeller has been stopped. Roosevelt continued to cut a large figure on the world stage. At the outset of the Russo-Japanese War, T.R. was pleased that the Japanese were scoring one success after another. Roosevelt had previously regarded Russia as the strongest single power in Asia. Now, he hoped, Japan would establish itself as Russia's equal. The two nations would then balance each other; neither would be able to expand. The situation itself would thus guarantee China's independence and territorial

John T. Morgan, who represented Alabama in the Senate for 30 years, doggedly campaigned for the Nicaraguan canal route and fought to exclude English participation. A peppery, self-taught man and an ex-Confederate general, he boasted that he had never set foot on a college campus until he used the walls of William and Mary as protection against Yankee bullets.

integrity, and the United States would be relieved of any need to mingle in Asian politics.

Not long after hostilities began, the Japanese started to think of a negotiated peace. As time passed, Roosevelt himself came to hope more and more strongly that a compromise peace could be worked out. Japanese victories followed one another, and Russia's defeats were compounded by unrest at home. Day by day it seemed more likely that, rather than establishing a Russo-Japanese equilibrium, the war would end with Japan dominating Eastern Asia.

Roosevelt had previously initiated talks designed to ensure friendship with a newly strengthened Japan. Through Secretary of War William Howard Taft, whom he sent to Japan in mid-1905, and through an unofficial envoy of the Japanese cabinet, Baron Kentaro Kaneko, he sought an informal understanding with Japan with regard to both countries' interests in the Far East. However, if Japan became all-powerful on the East Asian mainland, friction would be almost unavoidable. The Japanese would inevitably seek trade advantages. In all probability they would also take over some portions of China. Strongly committed to the Open Door policy and the territorial integrity of China, the United States would have to protest.

To avoid this possibility, Roosevelt had been pressing Russia to accept mediation. When Russia finally agreed, Roosevelt, anxious to avoid involvement, urged the plenipotentiaries to confer in Europe, then reluctantly bowed to Japanese insistence on an American meeting. But he sent the delegations to a hotel at Portsmouth, New Hampshire, and so kept them out of Washington.

Despite these tactics, Roosevelt did become involved, for the parties refused to come to terms until after he intervened several times to suggest concessions by one side or the other. Ironically enough, the reluctant peacemaker was awarded the Nobel Peace Prize in 1906 for his work in arranging the treaty. At least he could take comfort in the fact that, through his intervention, Japan and Russia still offset each other to some extent. There was reason to hope, therefore, that the situation in East Asia would remain stable.

IN the Moroccan crisis of 1905, Roosevelt's part was smaller and even more self-effacing. France's paramount position in Morocco had been recognized by England. But in a characteristically theatrical gesture, Kaiser Wilhelm II declared that Germany recognized only the sovereignty of the Moroccan sultan. The English supported the French demand that the Germans acknowledge French supremacy in Morocco; war seemed likely.

The Germans beseeched Roosevelt to arrange an international conference for discussion of Morocco. He refused. Then, fearful that a general European war was in prospect, Roosevelt agreed to use his influence with the French. Later the German ambassador in the United States, Speck von Sternburg, went somewhat beyond his instructions from Berlin and told Roosevelt that, if a conference met, the German delegates to it would abide by whatever recommendations the American government made to them.

Roosevelt informed the French of Speck's promise and, by intimating to them that he would support their views on the Moroccan question, obtained their consent to the calling of a conference. Although the German government was disconcerted when it discovered what Speck had told Roosevelt, it decided to abide by the pledge. The conference met at Algeciras, Spain, from January to April 1906. On the few issues that provoked serious dispute, the

This is the Nicaraguan stamp sent to U.S. congressmen by lobbyist Philippe Bunau-Varilla, whose company had taken over the old De Lesseps rights to the Panama route. By a fateful coincidence, this volcano, situated near the proposed Nicaraguan route, had erupted one month earlier, destroying the wharf seen in the foreground. Soon after, the Panama route was chosen.

Germans bowed to American recommendations, and the result was an agreement that temporarily reduced tension. Roosevelt's reputation as a peacemaker was higher than ever. Though he was proud of this fact, he was satisfied that the role he had played did not commit the United States to any responsibility for enforcement of the treaty.

Even in the Western Hemisphere, Roosevelt backed off from commitments. The Dominican Republic, in a situation similar to that of Venezuela before the Anglo-German-Italian intervention, owed large sums to foreign creditors and was either unable or unwilling to pay interest or principal. As European clamor mounted for a solution by force, Roosevelt felt the necessity to take some action. He arranged for American commissioners to take over administration of the Dominican customs and to use part of the receipts to pay off the country's debts, justifying this step with the proclamation in 1904 of what came to be called the "Roosevelt Corollary" to the Monroe Doctrine. He declared: "Chronic wrongdoing, or an impotence which results in a general loosening of the ties of civilized society, may in America, as elsewhere, ultimately require intervention by some civilized nation, and in the Western Hemisphere the adherence of the United States to the Monroe Doctrine may force the United States, however reluctantly, in flagrant cases of such wrongdoing or impotence, to the exercise of an international police power." In other words, Roosevelt announced that the United States would serve as sheriff for the hemisphere.

There was a fine imperialist ring to the corollary—it sounded as if the United States were declaring a protectorate over all Latin America. But despite the bold assertion of American prerogatives, Roosevelt took action under this declaration only by taking over Dominican customs collections in 1905. When trouble developed in Central America in 1906 and 1907, he was careful not to move on his own and acted only when Mexico agreed to a joint effort. In the Western Hemisphere as in Europe and Asia, Roosevelt's chief concern after the winter of 1903-1904 seemed to be to reduce and limit American commitments.

ALTHOUGH he tried, Roosevelt was not able to maintain tranquil relations with Japan. He ignored complaints by American consuls and businessmen about certain discriminatory trade practices by Japan. In 1908, moreover, his new Secretary of State, Elihu Root, signed with Japan an agreement that, in effect, recognized Japan's claim to special rights in Manchuria.

The sources of trouble were in the United States. Ever since the early 1890s Japanese immigrants had been coming in increasing numbers to California. By the beginning of 1906 as many as 1,000 were arriving every month, and California racists were up in arms. That year the San Francisco school board ordered that Japanese students should be put into a separate school. This example of prejudice and discrimination outraged the Japanese, and the Japanese government made a vigorous protest in Washington. In fact, education was locally controlled, California was a sovereign state and the federal government could do nothing except condemn the San Francisco decree, which Roosevelt did. This did not placate Japanese opinion. Feeling mounted in Japan, and reports of anti-Americanism there generated anti-Japanese feeling in the United States. Before long there was open talk on both sides of a possible war.

In this exaggerated cartoon, Roosevelt wields his big stick in Morocco, intervening in the dispute between Germany and the Anglo-French entente. T. R. was somewhat less than modest about his role in the affair: "You will notice that... I was most suave and pleasant with the [kaiser], yet when it became necessary... I stood him on his head with great decision."

War was the last thing Roosevelt wanted. Apart from broader considerations of policy, he was well aware that a war with Japan would be hard to fight. The Philippines, which he had so eagerly desired in 1898, he now regarded as America's "heel of Achilles." Military studies had demonstrated to him the difficulty of defending the islands against attack. Apart from strategic considerations, he had no sympathy with the California segregationists. Like most men of the time, he believed that some races were inferior to others, but he looked on the Japanese as one of the superior races. Roosevelt's one aim was to mollify the Japanese and end the crisis.

With characteristic energy, he invited a delegation of San Francisco officials to Washington and used on them all his arts of persuasion. In similar fashion he dealt with legislators from California who were talking belligerently of passing a law to forbid any further Japanese immigration. At the same time he explained to the Japanese candidly and in detail just what he could and could not accomplish.

Out of all these conversations, there came a compromise that satisfied all parties. The overwrought Western congressmen were persuaded to join Roosevelt in a successful plea to the San Francisco authorities to end segregation. In return the Japanese made a "Gentlemen's Agreement" to restrict emigration to the United States.

Baron Kentaro Kaneko, Japanese special diplomatic representative to the U.S., was an urbane aristocrat with a Harvard education. Baron Kaneko had been well liked by Theodore Roosevelt, who first met him at college. But in spite of their friendship, T. R. once cautioned an associate that Kaneko, while "a good fellow," was also "a fox, and a Japanese fox at that."

THIS crisis was followed, however, by another which, though briefer, was no less serious. Roosevelt himself precipitated it, and apparently he did so deliberately. Anti-American agitation in Japan was slow in dying down, and American newspapers continued to report instances as they occurred. Throughout the earlier negotiations, Roosevelt had used his influence to play down this sort of news. Then in the summer of 1907, he suddenly reversed course and began dropping hints that Japanese-American relations might take a sudden turn for the worse. All over the country front pages and editorial pages were soon alive with rumors of war.

In the midst of this furor, Roosevelt disclosed that the entire American battle fleet would move from the Atlantic to the Pacific. In the United States, in Japan and in Europe, the announcement stirred feverish speculation as to whether hostilities were imminent. After the fleet reached the Pacific, Roosevelt disclosed that it would make a circuit of the globe. He now spoke of a "good will cruise." The news that the fleet would visit Japan itself naturally aroused much comment. But as the ships continued on their way, the general atmosphere gradually changed. Anti-American demonstrations in Japan dropped off. When the fleet arrived in Japan, it was greeted not only cordially but festively.

Why did Roosevelt create the war scare? In all probability, he had four basic motives.

Roosevelt had repeatedly stated one reason—to test the fleet in a massive training exercise. A second was to give the Navy favorable publicity. Britain and Germany had recently started building dreadnoughts, super-battleships far superior to those of other nations. Roosevelt was convinced that the United States could be safe only if it had visible military and naval power sufficient to deter other nations from testing its strength. How else, for example, could the world know whether America was serious in telling others to keep hands off the Western Hemisphere? Congress, however, was economy-minded, so T.R. hoped to generate public enthusiasm for a dreadnought-building program through a successful cruise.

The third motive was more subtle. In the negotiations leading to the Gentlemen's Agreement, Roosevelt had shown intense eagerness for peace with Japan, and he may have feared that the Japanese had equated his desire for peace with a fear of war. In some future dispute they might assume that the threat of war could coerce the United States into capitulation. Roosevelt wanted to be sure that they made no such mistake. He was later to say that the round-the-world cruise had been his greatest contribution to peace. What he meant, probably, was that it served to deter Japan and other nations from putting the resoluteness of tne United States to a test.

Finally, there was a political motive. Although Roosevelt was pledged not to seek another term, he was most anxious that William Howard Taft, his chosen heir, should win the election. Since 1904, when Roosevelt had done well in the Far West, he had alienated a number of voters in that region. His conservation policies, which prevented the untrammeled exploitation of the natural resources of the West, had been noticeably unpopular on the Pacific slope and in the Rocky Mountain area. His stand on discrimination against Japanese had cost him still more support. His role in the Japanese war scare, followed by the fleet's impressive cruise, could regain some of his lost popularity in the West.

Roosevelt's reputation, high when he left office, has undergone several reappraisals. During the 1920s and 1930s, when pacifism was a strong current in American thought, there was a tendency to interpret him as a sword-rattler and blusterer. After World War II he came to be viewed as a realist, concerned with power relationships and the extent to which the United States had the physical means to achieve its ends.

The truth probably is that Roosevelt was something of a chauvinist, something of a hard-boiled politician, and many other things besides. He wanted the world to be aware of the might of the United States. On occasion, as in Panama and the round-the-world cruise, he used a display of force when he might have achieved his goals by diplomacy alone. But above all Roosevelt understood the relationship between policy and public opinion.

This last is the fact that emerges most clearly as Roosevelt's era recedes into better perspective. Roosevelt entered the presidency at a time when public interest in the world outside American boundaries seemed high. As time passed he saw this interest fading. At that point he might have persisted in enlarging the American sphere of action, hoping that in crises the public would back him. Instead he pulled back until the nation held only those positions—such as supremacy in the Caribbean—for which the people were clearly prepared to fight. Despite his fascination with international politics, Roosevelt was, above all, a politician sensitive to and representative of his constituents. And because it was what the public wanted, Roosevelt moved away from international involvement.

PRESIDENT TAFT, although willing to assume that the United States had important foreign interests, did not score significant successes in foreign policy. He and his Secretary of State, Philander C. Knox, made a number of ambitious starts—for example, they tried to persuade American financiers to build and finance railroads in Manchuria and Southern China in an effort to

Co-author of a monumental life of Lincoln, diplomat and cosmopolite, John Hay, Secretary of State under William McKinley and Theodore Roosevelt, was a man of many parts. Extremely popular, he was also a man of considerable reserve. Said one friend, "No matter how intimate you were, or how merry the occasion, nobody ever slapped John Hay on the back."

reduce Japanese control of those regions. Nothing came of this effort however.

From certain unfortunate phrases used by Taft, critics of the Administration developed the derogatory term "dollar diplomacy"—that is, they accused Taft and Knox of putting the government at the service of corporations and banks with foreign interests. Actually it was the other way around. Taft and Knox were constantly trying to convince American businessmen of the importance of foreign trade and overseas investment. The President felt that the United States had, or ought to have, far-flung interests; he and Knox became increasingly aware of what Roosevelt had perceived—that the public did not take these foreign interests seriously. Perhaps, Taft reasoned, if more American money were involved, public interest might increase. But he had little luck in accomplishing this end.

Hoping for at least one increase in foreign trade, Taft negotiated for tariff reciprocity with Canada. The Canadian Parliament refused its consent. Despite their best efforts, Taft and Knox could look back only on a series of defeats. At the end of Taft's Administration the United States still had no firm commitments outside the Western Hemisphere and few within it.

IN the 19th Century the United States had also been free of entanglements, but it had been regarded by others as a nation safely isolated. By the end of Taft's Administration the United States had to be taken into account by foreign statesmen when they weighed up the balances of power. This fact was soon to have important consequences.

Despite the arrogance and highhandedness Roosevelt had displayed at times, the British government had persevered in efforts to achieve better understanding with the United States. British statesmen declared emphatically that they would never do anything to jeopardize good relations. By 1905 the British had withdrawn nearly all their warships from Western Hemisphere waters, saying in effect that the Western Hemisphere was in the hands of the United States. With little active co-operation from Washington, the British government established a degree of understanding making it virtually certain that if a general European war broke out, the United States would be a friendly neutral.

France and Russia, Britain's probable allies in such a war, could make a similar assumption. To Britain's presumable enemies, Germany and Austria, America figured as a potentially hostile neutral, although the Germans, too, had made efforts to win American good will. The kaiser had, for example, sent his brother on a tour of the United States and presented a statue of Frederick the Great to the War Department. But the German government never gave American affairs the high priority the British did, and German-American relations steadily became worse rather than better. On very little evidence, Americans continued to suspect that Germany harbored a design to seize colonies in the Western Hemisphere. (One newspaper suggested that in repayment for the statue of Frederick, the United States should present Germany with a statue of James Monroe.)

Thus when war did break out, the role the United States would play was partly foreordained. After experimenting briefly with venturesome policies, the American government had pulled back somewhat. But nations, like individuals, can cut themselves off from others only with co-operation: They cannot let alone unless they are let alone. The United States was not to enjoy this luxury. In the end, it could not escape from the fact that it had become a great power.

This cartoon of 1900 on the Open Door policy, replete with the chauvinism of its time, lauds U.S. diplomacy as having unlocked "the riches of the flowery kingdom." Uncle Sam did not actually "open" China but he did try to obtain a competitive position for American merchants and traders and to keep Russia, England and others from taking more than their share.

With superb skill, one man guides the 33 horses pulling a harvester. This was 1902, and tractors would end the horse's reign within 25 years.

Twilight of American innocence

THE American scene, from the turn of the century until the United States entered World War I, was in a state of continuing, if not headlong transition. For example, in 1900 the word "horsepower," generally used to measure motive power, might refer to such awesome collections of equine muscle as the 33-horse team above. But only nine years later, six times that much power could be contained under the hood of a single racing car *(opposite)*.

The period began with a feeling of almost smug satisfaction with things as they were. Populist thunderclaps had subsided to a distant, almost inaudible muttering. People scoffed at the "horseless carriage" and dismissed the Wright brothers' first plane flight as some sort of trickery. The very rich believed themselves the beneficiaries of a kind of principle of natural selection, which absolved them of any concern—much less responsibility—for the tragic plight of exploited labor. But things were stirring. The automobile, along with the airplane, would not be put off, any more so than the inevitable revelation that women had ankles beneath all those voluminous skirts. And it was becoming apparent that the ladies had calves as well. And strong lungs, too, that powered their increasingly vociferous demand of "Votes for Women!" The sunny days of America's age of innocence were drawing to a close.

DEATH-DEFYING RACERS hurtle past a nonchalant girl in this 1909 poster for the Indianapolis Speedway's first season. Then, as now, the lure of danger drew crowds.

Indianapolis Motor Speedway

GREATEST RACE COURSE IN THE WORLD

Management
C. G. FISHER   F. H. WHEELER
A. C. NEWBY   J. A. ALLISON

GALLANTLY CRANKING, a good Samaritan risks a broken arm to start this stalled Packard. The Kettering self-starter, invented in 1911, somewhat reduced the hazards and delays of motoring.

BLOWOUT pits man against machine, with machine obviously the victor. Here an annoyed motorist of 1908 sorts through his spare tires, while the women inspect the cause of the blowout.

A quintet of vintage cars from the Henry Ford Museum, Dearborn, Michigan, includes (from left) a 1910 Oldsmobile Ltd., a three-wheeled

From rich man's toy to indispensable vehicle

No disaster, depression or war had as much of an impact on American manners and morals as did the automobile revolution. And the years between 1900 and 1917 were perhaps the most significant in the automobile's meteoric rise from novelty to necessity. The 8,000 cars registered in 1900 were chiefly playthings for the wealthy—cranky, open-air affairs (some of which are shown below) subject, among a host of ailments, to frequent tire trouble *(left)*. By 1917, there were some 4,700,500 loose on the streets (an increase of more than 58,600 per cent), and they were reasonably reliable, reasonably weather-tight and sold, new, for as little as $345, F.O.B. Detroit. In 1913 Henry Ford had introduced the moving assembly-line production technique (itself no small contribution to the American scene).

By 1919 most models sported self-starters as an optional extra, which pleased everybody except perhaps physicians, who had done a thriving business treating "starter's arm," a fracture of the forearm caused by unexpected kickbacks of the starting crank.

All this time the automobile was making its mark, despite a paucity of repair shops and gasoline stations, over inadequate roads. The first cross-country trip was completed in 1903 in 52 days. Five years later, six cars set forth in a race westward across the world from New York to Paris. It proved to be more of an endurance contest. From Wyoming to the West Coast, passable roads were conspicuously absent. And Siberia was one mass of trackless terrain. But three of the starters made it—the winner taking five months and 18 days.

1896 Duryea, a 1909 Chalmers Detroit roadster (in the doorway), a 1910 Stanley Steamer and "Old Pacific," a one-cylinder 1903 Packard.

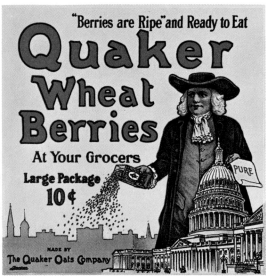

A noted opera singer, a Quaker scattering oats on the Capitol and a placid Dutch boy advertise products renowned in 1905—and today.

Uneeda's boy in a slicker recalls years of Nabisco ads

The hard-sell times of uninhibited advertising

ADVERTISING in the years before 1900 saw the hard sell at its rowdiest. Copywriters were constrained only by their inhibitions, which seemed in very short supply indeed. Patent-medicine ads promised cures for everything from freckles to drug addiction, along with such maladies as "blood poverty," which even doctors had rarely heard of. If one believed the ads, a man could "insure love and a happy home" by taking one nostrum or another. If these remedies failed, there were always the ads for mail-order divorces—bogus, of course. Public indignation against this avalanche of misrepresentation finally spurred the passage of the federal Pure Food and Drug Act in 1906.

Almost simultaneously, the rise of nationally circulated magazines gave manufacturers the medium they needed to push mass sales. A parallel development was the burgeoning of symbols that would be uniquely identifiable with a particular product. Dozens of trademarks blossomed, often drawn from unlikely sources. The dromedary which still adorns the Camel cigarette package used as its model a moth-eaten Barnum & Bailey veteran named Old Joe. Some of these trademarks of the early 1900s—like the child *(opposite)* sitting on a cake of Fairy Soap—are today as extinct as the passenger pigeon. But others, like "His Master's Voice" *(above, opposite)*, remain familiar, having triumphed over Madison Avenue's constant search for novelty. The rainproof young man at the left rescued the soda cracker from the general store's barrel and became so famous that he was warmly remembered for years after his last appearance.

134

This famous trademark, the survivor of six decades of corporate change, comes from a painting in which the dog's master lies in his coffin.

DAILY CLEANLINESS, early in this century still a relatively new idea, is the message of this ad for soap. Child models were supposed to appeal to the maternal instinct of housewives.

Here, the product being sold is presumably hard at work.

A 1910 clothier's notice features two collegians.

135

CHARMINGLY BACKLIGHTED, a young boy pensively blows soapy bubbles in an early autochrome taken by Arnold Genthe.

PROUDLY POSED, a honeymoon couple sits for a color portrait on a rock in New York's Van Cortlandt Park around 1912. Developed in Europe in 1903, autochromes used glass plates coated with dyed starch which registered color when processed.

Early efforts of adventurous color photographers

IN the serene years when the public was learning the joys of the motor car and the pleasures of drinking Coca-Cola, photography was a far cry—via the ubiquitous Kodak camera—from the dark ages of the daguerreotype. A pioneering school of New York cameramen headed by Alfred Stieglitz, a photographer and art sponsor, was actually championing photography as a serious art form and was composing pictures in a romantic mood. In September 1907 the Stieglitz group passed an important milestone when it showed a collection of the first practical color photographs, called "autochromes," ever taken in this country. Some sample autochromes are shown on these pages. Quite apart from their technical significance, the pictures themselves are historically important, for they capture, in almost living color, the restful temper so common in the early 20th Century.

LANGUIDLY ARRANGED, a group decorates the porch of a summer place, perhaps in upstate New York. The date of this autochrome is unknown, but the clothing points to the early 1900s.

BROODINGLY ENSCONCED, Alfred Stieglitz' sister Selma poses for a color portrait by her brother. Taken about 1907, it is probably one of the earliest autochromes shot in America.

A long-brewing revolt of American womanhood

At the dawn of the 20th Century, the lid which kept women in their place was still on—but just barely so. Although Abigail Adams had long ago fought to include women's emancipation in the Constitution, men had successfully defended their supremacy for more than a century. Now, fired by the efforts of women like feminist Susan B. Anthony and social worker Jane Addams *(opposite)*, the woman's rights movement gathered momentum. The low hemlines rose, and daring "peekaboo" blouses appeared. Even exercise won approval *(below)*, along with the right to work. In 1870, there were 930 women office workers in the whole U.S. By 1910 the number of these female workers had soared to 386,765.

PENCIL IN HAIR, this secretary is one of the many girls who, safe in the knowledge that "heaven will protect the working girl," risked big-city life to make a living in the early 1900s.

DUMBBELLS IN THE AIR, a determined, primly coiffed and bloomered YWCA gym class works out. Physical fitness, perhaps for self-protection, was stressed by the feminists.

Jane Addams (far right), a leader of the fight for woman's rights, stands with two aides in a touring car during a suffragette parade.

7. THE
ROAD
TO WAR

WOODROW WILSON'S convictions on foreign policy were unlike those of any of his immediate predecessors. Albeit in different ways, McKinley, Theodore Roosevelt and Taft had all concerned themselves with American national interests. They had acted on the assumption that the United States was engaged in competition with other nations—for trade, power or at least prestige. Wilson, on the other hand, assumed that the United States had no interests except such as were common to all mankind. He believed that America should never pursue selfish ends but should always keep before it the ideal of serving humanity. In Wilson's view America's primary role was to guide the world's onward march to democracy. His outlook was that of a missionary.

From the very beginning he and his Secretary of State, William Jennings Bryan, gave American diplomacy a new tone. Taft had pressed the great New York banks to join in an international loan to China. Wilson opposed the loan because the strings attached to this loan would affect China's administrative independence. When a crisis developed with Japan over a California law forbidding Japanese to own land there, military experts recommended precautionary fleet movements, but the President told reporters that the very idea of war was preposterous.

In the State Department, Bryan introduced a new informality. He would see almost anyone who called. True to his prohibitionist beliefs, he refused to serve wine at his official dinners, occasionally substituting grape juice. He

A STAUNCH IDEALIST, Woodrow Wilson seems more professor than President in this portrait, but in the White House he was surprisingly at ease in the political arena.

devoted himself heart and soul to negotiating bilateral treaties that bound the signatory nations, after failure to resolve disputes by diplomacy, to submit their quarrels to a board of inquiry for a "cooling-off" period of six months to a year, during which time they would not go to war. Bryan actually completed 30 such treaties (none of which would ever be invoked), celebrating each with the presentation to the other signer of a paperweight replica of a plowshare beaten from a sword, in token of a stride taken toward perpetual peace.

Despite Uncle Sam's disapproval, President Huerta clings to his hold on Mexico. By 1913 dealings with Huerta had become so difficult that Wilson sent a personal agent to investigate. Meanwhile the State Department sent a secret agent. Then, in a farcical confrontation, the two agents and the bewildered U.S. ambassador came face-to-face with each other in Mexico City.

NOT all New Freedom diplomacy was unorthodox. In the Caribbean, for example, the Administration found itself heir to problems very similar to those previous Presidents had faced. Affairs in Haiti and Santo Domingo became so turbulent that Washington felt that the alternatives were to intervene or to let absolute chaos reign. Wilson ordered Marines into both countries and set up occupation regimes which, as it turned out, continued for years. But he added a Wilsonian touch that distinguished his policy from Roosevelt's or Taft's. In both Haiti and Santo Domingo, Wilson kept trying to get politicians to hold free elections and abide by the results. The ironic result of his efforts was to push conditions from bad to worse.

The main focus of Wilson's missionary effort was Mexico. Almost upon taking office in March 1913, Wilson had an opportunity to put his beliefs into practice. Two years earlier Mexico had finally had a forward-looking revolution that dispossessed the ruling oligarchy. Then Victoriano Huerta, a cruel, shrewd and reactionary general, took power after a counterrevolution climaxed by the assassination of President Francisco I. Madero in February 1913. Feeling that the cause of democracy and liberalism had suffered a setback, Wilson was saddened. His sorrow turned to dismay when he began to suspect that Taft's ambassador to Mexico, Henry Lane Wilson, had had a hand in bringing Huerta to power. Reports from special agents confirmed that the ambassador had at least been aware of the conspiracy to overthrow Madero and may even have approved the Huerta-sponsored murder.

To show his disapproval, Wilson refused to extend the customary *de facto* recognition to Huerta. He hoped Huerta's regime would topple. It did not. On the contrary, Huerta gained added strength. Wilson became even more determined to bring about Huerta's downfall. He had embargoed shipments of arms to Mexico in August. In February 1914 he lifted the embargo in order to let munitions reach Venustiano Carranza and Francisco ("Pancho") Villa, who were the leaders of the armed opposition to Huerta.

Still the dictator held on. In April 1914 American sailors went ashore at Tampico and were arrested by a *Huertista* colonel. Although Mexican officials promptly ordered their release and apologized, the American commanding officer demanded punishment of the colonel and a 21-gun salute to the American flag. Huerta apologized and offered to punish the officer if he were found to have acted improperly. Mexican guns, he said, would salute the American flag if American guns saluted Mexico's. These proposals seemed conciliatory, and many in the Administration believed the matter could be settled.

Not so the President. It was evident that Carranza and Villa were not gaining ground. But Wilson was determined that Huerta should knuckle under. The American Navy was ordered to close in on the Mexican coasts, plans were drawn up for landings at Tampico and Veracruz and for the possible dispatch of an expedition to Mexico City. Upon learning that a shipload of munitions was due to arrive at Veracruz from Europe, Wilson ordered the port seized.

One thousand sailors and Marines went ashore on April 21, 1914. They met resistance only as they advanced into the city. Another 3,000 landed; 19 were killed and 71 wounded. By noon on April 22 the occupation was complete. But Wilson, who had expected no opposition, was shocked by the casualties.

Still more unsettling for him was evidence of the reaction among the Mexican people, who seemed to rally to Huerta once again. Even the *Carranzistas* said they would fight against an American invasion of their country. Instead of being acclaimed as saviors of democracy, American troops were reviled as enemies. Wilson found that he was on the verge of a war that might be long, bloody, bitter and not necessarily just. He decided to retreat. He canceled all plans for a blockade and further landings, ordered the American commander at Veracruz to take no action that might heighten tensions, and accepted an Argentine-Brazilian-Chilean proposal for mediation. At Niagara Falls American delegates conferred with envoys of the very government that Wilson had so long refused to recognize. He did not altogether abandon his earlier hopes. As a condition for a reconciliation, he still insisted on Huerta's resignation. In July 1914 Wilson at last had the satisfaction of learning that Huerta would abdicate and go into exile. But Carranza, the new leader of Mexico, proved no more amenable to American advice than had Huerta. Pancho Villa was now fighting Carranza, and although Villa was nothing but a bandit with delusions of grandeur, Wilson convinced himself that Villa was a rough-hewn reformer. From Villa's hypocritical protestations, the President reasoned that American help would make the bandit receptive to guidance from Washington. Fortunately, before becoming entangled in another Veracruz affair, Wilson realized that Carranza was much more popular and powerful than he had supposed. With considerable reluctance he decided to make his peace with Carranza.

It was not easy to do. Discussions between Washington and Mexico City dragged on. Meanwhile Villa made trouble by crossing the Rio Grande and staging a raid on American soil. Carranza at last agreed to let United States troops pursue Villa back across the border. But, given an inch, General John J. Pershing led 7,000 American soldiers 300 miles into Mexico. To Carranza this was practically an invasion, and he demanded that the troops be pulled back. Many Americans clamored for a military invasion to pacify Mexico. In the summer of 1916 war seemed a certainty.

But by this time Wilson only wanted to get out of Mexico without loss of face, and Carranza was wise enough to know that if war came, Mexico would be the loser. The two presidents fenced with one another, making enough compromises so that negotiations could continue. That winter, when the United States faced a crisis of incomparably greater magnitude, Wilson ordered Pershing's men back and settled outstanding issues.

IN the Mexican episode Wilson had suffered one defeat after another. However in the end he got more or less what he had wanted. Carranza established a regime that, if not thoroughly democratic, was at least popularly backed. While American interventions and threats had probably only delayed this result, observers at the time could well have felt that Wilson's "missionary diplomacy" had been a success. Now this program was to be tried on a much larger scale in an effort to extend democracy to the whole world.

On June 28, 1914, Archduke Franz Ferdinand of Austria-Hungary had been

Woodrow Wilson, shown above in a 1912 caricature, took an attitude of "watchful waiting" toward the Mexican civil war. His efforts to develop a policy inspired varied comments: some assailed him for being too aggressive, others said that he was not aggressive enough. One wag composed the "Wilson Tango": "one step forward, two steps backward, side-step, hesitate."

assassinated in Sarajevo. This event had set off a chain of events that within a few months engulfed all Europe in what was to become known as the Great War or the World War.

At the outset American reactions were mixed. Some people, mostly German-Americans, took the side of Austria and Germany. Probably a majority favored the alliance of Russia, France and Britain. Although cultural ties with England undoubtedly accounted for some of this sympathy, Germany's violation of Belgian neutrality to strike at France had profoundly shocked and alienated American opinion. German Chancellor Theobald von Bethmann-Hollweg's contemptuous description of the solemn treaty of neutrality as a mere "scrap of paper" was widely quoted with disapproval. German atrocities in Belgium horrified Americans. Many agreed with Allied propagandists that the war was one between civilization and barbarism.

Nearly everyone had assumed that the war would be short. But after the near miracle on the Marne that checked the German drive against Paris in September 1914, a stalemate developed on the Western Front. It became clear that fighting might go on for months (perhaps even years), and the passions of most Americans cooled. Cases arose in which the Allies, too, paid scant attention to international law. Invoking dubious rules, the British stopped American ships on the high seas and took them into their ports to be searched for contraband; as in the past, Americans were touchy about freedom of the seas. Nevertheless, most Americans regarded the Allies as morally the better. The commonest attitude, however, was a mixture of relief at not being involved and conviction that none of the issues in the conflict concerned America. At the outbreak of the war, President Wilson had felt it necessary to exhort his countrymen to remain "impartial in thought as well as in action."

The Administration made it its business to see that nothing disturbed this mood of noninvolvement. At first the chief threat to continuing American neutrality seemed to be that of disputes with the British over neutral rights—disputes that might get out of hand as they had in 1812. To avoid this possibility became the chief business of certain key advisers. Walter Hines Page, the American ambassador in London, who wanted the United States to support England in the war, on more than one occasion actually helped the British government reply to complaints from Washington.

ALTHOUGH Page's conduct was the most extreme, other men, from the President down, were equally intent on preventing trouble. Colonel Edward M. House, the President's closest friend and adviser, wanted the Allies to win but hoped that their victory would not be so great as to destroy Germany as a counterweight to Russia on the Continent. The chief legal officer of the State Department, Robert Lansing, held somewhat similar views to Ambassador Page. Recalling the exchange of diplomatic correspondence between Britain and the United States, Lansing later wrote: "The notes that were sent were long and exhaustive treatises which opened up new subjects of discussion rather than closing those in controversy. . . . Everything was submerged in verbosity. It was done with deliberate purpose. It insured continuance of the controversies and left the questions unsettled."

Nonetheless these notes were stiffly legalistic, and they could have led to trouble. However, British concessions indicated an equal determination to preserve Anglo-American friendship. Americans prospered by exports to Eu-

THE FRUSTRATING CHASE
OF AN ELUSIVE BANDIT

After Pancho Villa raided a U.S. Army town (1), Pershing set out to capture him. Dividing his troops into small, mobile units, he pursued the smaller, more mobile guerrillas. One of his forays (short black arrows) was nearly successful: 400 troopers had Villa surrounded (2). Villa escaped in a hair-raising chase over the mountains. Mexicans resented the American "invaders" more than they did Villa, so they drubbed Yankee troops out of two towns (3 and 4). Dotted lines show retreats; the area in which these actions occurred is located in the inset.

ropean neutrals and by selling goods and lending money to the Allies. A clash with the Germans seemed unlikely, for they did not control the high seas. As of January 1915, Washington expected that the United States would sit out the war comfortably, living up to Jefferson's injunction that the New World should "fatten on the follies of the old."

O N February 4, 1915, however, the Germans suddenly announced that submarines would sink without warning any Allied ships found in the waters around the British Isles. Pointing out that submarines would not necessarily be able to distinguish between Allied and neutral vessels, the German government urged neutral states to keep their ships out of the zone.

Wilson was incredulous. The submarine was a relatively new weapon, whose use in enforcing a blockade had hardly been thought of. Undersea raiders first showed they could execute independent missions when two German U-boats sank four British ships in the North Sea in September 1914. To young German naval officers, frustrated by the glory won by the army, the sinkings suggested a concerted campaign against merchantmen. Admiral Alfred von Tirpitz, the grand old man of the German navy, publicly endorsed this idea and thus gave it some publicity. But if Wilson had read of it, it is likely that he had dismissed it as Allied propaganda. Accepted practice permitted belligerents to stop enemy merchantmen and inspect their papers and, in exceptional circumstances, to sink them after first insuring the safety of crew and passengers. In the case of neutral vessels, the rule was that contraband could be removed, after which the ship could proceed. To Wilson it seemed absolutely unthinkable that the German government should now discard this tradition and threaten neutral shipping and lives.

Lansing felt that the Germans had to be reproached in strong language, and he and the President quickly drew up a note warning that if an American were killed or an American ship sunk, the United States would consider it "an indefensible violation of neutral rights." In such an event, "the United States would be constrained to hold the Imperial German Government to a strict accountability . . . and to take any steps it might be necessary to take." This was the toughest language that diplomacy permitted.

The Germans replied at length, promising that they would try to keep neutral ships from harm. Without formal notification to Washington, the submarine offensive against Allied shipping was postponed and then recommenced under such stringent restrictions that its initial results were unspectacular.

But if Wilson felt elation, as he was perhaps entitled to, it was short-lived. April brought reports of increasing submarine activity. An American citizen had died in the torpedoing of a British passenger liner, the *Falaba*. Since he had been on a belligerent ship in a war zone, the case was somewhat ambiguous. Lansing and most of Wilson's advisers felt it violated American rights. Since Bryan thought otherwise, the President—who was of two minds—deferred action. On May 1 an American ship, the *Gulflight*, was torpedoed, though not sunk. In the panic that followed, three Americans died. This was a very serious incident, but the events of the next week quickly turned attention from the *Gulflight*.

On May 7 at 3 in the afternoon, a cablegram reached Washington from the United States embassy in London: "The *Lusitania* was torpedoed off the Irish Coast and sunk in half an hour." One of the largest and most luxurious

Secretary of State Bryan struts between Pancho Villa and Venustiano Carranza in this satirical cartoon, "The Three Musketeers." Of the two Mexican revolutionaries, Bryan considered Villa the "idealist" because he did not smoke or drink. At a time when some American papers labeled Villa "a robber, a murderer, and a rapist," Bryan called him "a Sir Galahad."

liners afloat, the *Lusitania* had sailed from New York on May 1. Among its 1,257 passengers were many prominent Americans. Despite the war, and regardless of the German embassy's warning in New York papers that the British ship was sailing into a war zone, social life aboard ship had been as gay as ever. Although the captain of the *Lusitania* had instructions to steer a zigzag course in the war zone as protection against submarines, he disregarded them, partly because he could not believe that his ship would be attacked.

The torpedo struck the starboard bow and apparently blew up a boiler. The giant vessel at once began to heel and sink. In the quarter hour before it went under, there was a frantic rush to the lifeboats. Some 700 got away. But 1,198 passengers and crewmen died, 128 of them Americans.

IN Washington almost everyone felt the time had come to hold Germany to the "strict accountability" promised by Wilson. But Bryan, now desperately fearful of war, saw points on the German side. The *Lusitania* had carried munitions; the dead passengers had knowingly taken a risk that they could have avoided. But few others in the Administration sympathized with this reasoning. The Germans, most agreed, had committed a barbarous crime and would have to pay for it.

Wilson went into almost complete seclusion to decide what he should do. Three days later, in a speech before a group of newly naturalized citizens, he declared: "There is such a thing as a man being too proud to fight. There is such a thing as a nation being so right that it does not need to convince others by force that it is right."

These words provoked fierce criticism from segments of the press, Congress and the public. However the note that Wilson sent to Berlin on May 13 was firmer than might have been expected. It demanded an apology, reparations and assurances that no such incident would recur. To comply, Germany would have to abandon any undersea warfare against merchant shipping.

When Berlin's answer arrived, 18 days later, it was unsatisfactory, for it practically justified the sinking on grounds similar to those argued by Bryan. Countering the American demands, Germany proposed that the United States enter into prolonged investigation of and debate about whether the *Lusitania* had carried munitions, had orders to sink submarines on sight and other matters. Wilson was in a quandary. He had meant every word in his first *Lusitania* note. On the other hand, he had a horror of the obvious alternatives to acceptance of the German position—the severance of diplomatic relations or a message to Congress proposing a declaration of war. Feeling in the country was obviously calmer than it had been immediately after the sinking, and Bryan and a few others in the Administration, citing the more moderate climate of public and congressional opinion, were frantically pleading for retreat.

Wilson concluded that the best course was merely to reiterate what he had said earlier and, while offering the Germans further time for consideration, to make clear to them that he insisted on action. Although the Secretary of State had signed the first *Lusitania* note, he balked at the second. Bryan wanted a frank declaration that the United States would press for arbitration, even if the case had to wait until peace returned. He also wanted to warn American citizens not to sail on belligerent vessels in the war zone. Finally, he urged the President to couple any new note to Berlin with an equally stern note protesting British violation of neutral rights. Such a note,

CUNARD

EUROPE VIA LIVERPOOL
LUSITANIA
Fastest and Largest Steamer
now in Atlantic Service Sails
SATURDAY, MAY 1, 10 A. M.
Transylvania, Fri., May 7, 5 P.M.
Orduna, ⋅ ⋅ Tues., May 18, 10 A.M.
Tuscania, ⋅ ⋅ Fri., May 21, 5 P.M.
LUSITANIA, Sat., May 29, 10 A.M.
Transylvania, Fri., June 4, 5 P.M.

Gibraltar—Genoa—Naples—Piraeus
S.S. Carpathia, Thur., May 13, Noon

Next to the Cunard announcement in New York papers (above), the German embassy published a warning (below). Although mysterious telegrams warned prominent passengers against sailing, no one took them seriously. Newsreel cameramen, filming the departing travelers, scoffed at the risk by shouting: "We're going to call this 'The "Lusitania's" Last Voyage!'"

NOTICE!
TRAVELLERS intending to embark on the Atlantic voyage are reminded that a state of war exists between Germany and her allies and Great Britain and her allies; that the zone of war includes the waters adjacent to the British Isles; that, in accordance with formal notice given by the Imperial German Government, vessels flying the flag of Great Britain, or of any of her allies, are liable to destruction in those waters and that travellers sailing in the war zone on ships of Great Britain or her allies do so at their own risk.

IMPERIAL GERMAN EMBASSY
WASHINGTON, D. C., APRIL 22, 1915.

146

he thought, would demonstrate America's genuine commitment to neutrality.

Wilson was tempted by a few of Bryan's suggestions, and he gave tentative approval to the idea of releasing an unofficial but authoritative statement that the government intended to negotiate a settlement by diplomatic methods. But Wilson was dissuaded by other advisers who pointed out that such a statement might discourage any German efforts at conciliation. When Wilson reluctantly turned down all of his Secretary's proposals, Bryan was distraught. It was clear to him he could not change Wilson's mind. Nor, in conscience, could Bryan endorse the policy that Wilson obviously meant to follow.

According to his wife, Bryan began to come home from his office "with bloodshot eyes and weary steps." At night he would toss and lie awake. By early June Wilson was writing apologetically: "You always have such weight of reason, as well as such high motives, behind what you urge that it is with deep misgiving that I turn from what you press on me." But, Wilson said, he saw no way to avoid "hopelessly weakening our protest." Just before the note went off, Bryan came to the White House. With a quiver in his voice, he told the President that he saw no alternative but to resign.

A long, sad conversation followed—Presbyterian elder speaking to Presbyterian elder the language of moral duty, one generation of Democratic leadership addressing the other. Neither man was converted. Bryan went home to compose a letter saying, "To remain a member of the Cabinet would be as unfair to you as it would be to the cause which is nearest my heart, namely, the prevention of war." Wilson accepted the resignation "with much more than deep regret, with a feeling of personal sorrow." He went on: "Our judgments have accorded in practically every matter of official duty and of public policy.... Even now we are not separated in the object we seek, but only in the method by which we seek it." Bryan's resignation took effect on June 8.

O N the following day the second *Lusitania* note went off by cable to Germany. Reiterating earlier demands, it warned: "The Government of the United States is contending for something much greater than mere rights of property or privileges of commerce. It is contending for nothing less high and sacred than the rights of humanity."

The Germans again delayed answering, and when their response finally came it was once more disputatious and inconclusive. But meanwhile secret orders went out to submarine commanders to refrain from attacking passenger-carrying vessels. Wilson saw that his essential demand had, in effect, been met, and he was content not to insist upon more. "Apparently the Germans *are* modifying their methods," he wrote to Colonel House. "They must be made to feel that they must continue in their new way unless they deliberately wish to prove to us that they are unfriendly and wish war."

This was the line Wilson followed consistently. In August 1915, after there had been some revival of submarine activity, another passenger liner, the *Arabic*, was sunk. Wilson protested again. Despite the impatience of the press and some of his closest advisers, he gave the German government time to consider, and he won from it a public admission that, since the *Lusitania* exchanges, submarine commanders had been given secret orders not to attack large passenger-carrying vessels without warning.

There was another lull. Then in the spring of 1916, a French steamer, the *Sussex*, was torpedoed. This time Wilson dispatched a virtual ultimatum.

First reports (above) indicated that most of the "Lusitania's" passengers had survived the German torpedoing—but 1,198 of the 1,924 aboard had died. The enormous toll aroused violent anger in the U.S., but the sinking fanned patriotic pride in Germany. A German club struck off a medal (below) which shows Death gloating over the "Foolhardy, forewarned" victims.

He went before Congress to declare solemnly that diplomatic relations would be severed unless Germany abandoned submarine attacks on passenger and freight vessels. From Berlin came a pledge that ships would not be sunk without warning or without provision for the safety of passengers and crew. Out of these crises Wilson had pulled one diplomatic triumph after another.

On no occasion did the outcome of one crisis ensure against the occurrence of another. The first note to Germany, speaking of "strict accountability," had been vague. Had the Germans ignored it and pursued a ruthless submarine campaign, Wilson could have said, without serious loss of face, that he meant only to hold them accountable after the war was over. Nor did the first *Lusitania* note foreclose the possibility of temporizing. But after that the prestige of the nation was at stake. If the Germans disregarded America's views, the President would either have to back up his words with action or make the humiliating admission that he had been bluffing.

This had been the significance of his differences with Bryan. The Secretary had advocated moderation because, as he said, the President's policy could start a reaction that would "rush us into war in spite of anything we could do." In one of his letters to Wilson, Bryan declared, "If the initiative were with us, I would not fear war for I am sure you do not want it, but when the note is sent it is Germany's next move. . . ."

Wilson decided to take this risk. He was so sure that the American position was morally right, and so hopeful that on reflection the Germans would accept it, that he set before them the choice between doing as he asked and inviting war. For some time to come, this policy was successful. But the choice was still Germany's. As the fighting in Europe settled into an interminable pattern of butchery, as weary anger grew, the danger mounted that the Germans might decide for war.

THERE was another possibility. The United States might escape the choice between humiliation and war if the European war were to end in a negotiated peace. Wilson had long dreamed of such a solution. During the crisis of August 1914, he had offered good offices. At the time of the battle of the Marne, he had let Bryan make inquiries about the aims of the two sides and the possibilities for mediation. From the Allies, however, had come the reply that no peacemaking would be tolerated until German militarism was destroyed. Colonel House warned him that any pressure for peace would be considered unfriendly by London and would make it much harder for the Allied governments to be conciliatory in disputes about neutral rights. Impressed by this advice, Wilson decided to confine talk of mediation to private and unofficial conferences conducted by House.

In 1915, even before the submarine issue arose, Wilson sent Colonel House to Europe to sound out feeling on a negotiated peace. A slight, gray, soft-spoken Texan with an honorary colonelcy, Edward Mandell House had turned from business at an early age to devote himself to Texas politics. Then he moved on to an interest in progressive politics on the national scene. He sought out Wilson shortly before the nominating convention of 1912. Out of their meeting, there developed an extraordinarily intimate relationship. House became the man with whom the President shared his most private thoughts, his acidulous opinions of certain men in Washington, his doubts, his hopes and his ambitions. Wilson looked on House as his other self,

President Woodrow Wilson and his new wife campaigned together in 1916. Mrs. Wilson, a stunning woman with lustrous dark hair, brought out a boyishness in her austere husband which astonished his associates. The morning after the wedding, a Secret Service man found the President dancing and singing: "Oh you beautiful doll, You great big beautiful doll!"

trusted him utterly and assumed that in any situation House would speak and act as he would himself.

For the 1915 mission, House seemed a perfect choice. Just before the war broke out he had made friends in high places in European capitals. House was a listener rather than a talker, and, according to Sir Edward Grey, the British Foreign Secretary, "he had a way of saying 'I know it' in a tone and manner that carried conviction both of his sympathy with, and understanding of, what was said to him." If any man could find out about the prospects for peacemaking without causing offense, House could do so. He did. But the word he sent back was simply that it was not yet time for peace. The Allies wanted victories before talking, and the Germans dreamed of imposing conqueror's terms. It was best for the President to remain silent.

Three Americans died when the "Laconia," a British vessel, was torpedoed February 25, 1917, by a German U-boat. An irate cartoon in New York's "Evening World" shouted: "Without Warning!" The New York "Times," in a firm tone, stated: "Casuistry cannot disguise nor ingenuity palliate the crime of the German submarine commander who sank the 'Laconia.' "

EARLY in 1916 Wilson suggested that House make another trip to Europe. The *Arabic* crisis was then past, and Wilson was concerned that unless peace were restored, another similar confrontation might end with America in the war. Moreover, House had suggested a daring plan. On the assumption that a clash with Germany was inevitable if the war did not end, House proposed that Wilson tell the Allies that he intended to demand a mediated peace. If either group of belligerents refused to participate in peacemaking, the United States would join the other. The Allies would be asked to disclose confidentially the terms of peace they would accept, and Wilson would then propose a peace to the Germans on these conditions. On this basis, House thought, the Allies could have no objection to mediation, for they would be guaranteed the peace they wanted or, failing that, the active aid of the United States. If the Germans then accepted Wilson's demand, peace might be restored. If not, America would be in the war with a positive objective, not merely by reason of the submarine campaign.

In possession of Wilson's provisional approval of this plan, House carefully broached the idea in London, went on to Germany, where he satisfied himself that an all-out submarine campaign was not far off, and returned to England to sign with Sir Edward Grey one of the most extraordinary documents in American history. It said that Wilson would, "on hearing from France and England that the moment was opportune . . . propose that a Conference . . . be summoned to put an end to the war. Should the Allies accept this proposal, and should Germany refuse it, the United States would probably enter the war against Germany."

Since he was a private citizen, House's signature had no binding effect on the United States. But after House returned he secured Wilson's approval and then cabled the news to Grey. The House-Grey understanding, once endorsed by Wilson, constituted a secret agreement to bring the United States into the war. Wilson had made only one change in the secret memorandum, now an official document: He said the United States would "probably" go to war. Obviously the "probably" referred to the fact that Congress, not he, had the constitutional power to declare war.

Nothing came of it. The British regarded its terms as minimal and hoped that much more might be won if they pressed on to victory. On the other hand, if negotiations were to begin at that moment, when the German military position was so favorable, the British felt they might not even achieve their minimal terms. Despite repeated promptings from Washington, they never gave the required signal to call a conference. Wilson, additionally vexed by the Royal Navy's increasing interruption of neutral trade, burst out to House that the British had been "blindly stupid."

The time was rapidly approaching when Wilson would have to submit his first term's achievements to the test of national elections. With regard to the President's German policy, the country was of several minds. During the arguments over the second *Lusitania* note, Bryan had learned that there was strong antiwar sentiment in Congress. However, there was also a powerful current of opinion, especially strong in the urban Northeast, in favor of firmer opposition to the Germans. Theodore Roosevelt was loudly critical of what he termed Wilson's "milk and water" policy. The Army League and the Navy League were loudly propagandizing in favor of preparedness for war.

F ROM the end of 1914 on, there had been widespread German subversion and sabotage in America—enough to justify several sensational trials and official requests by the American government for recall of a number of German and Austrian diplomats implicated in these incidents. People in Eastern cities who remained pro-German were likely to be regarded as unpatriotic. But even among people who thought of Germany as an enemy, there were few who felt that immediate action was called for. As for the submarine issue, the most widespread attitude appeared to be a mixture of approval for Wilson's stand, delight that the American government could make Germany back down and doubt that attacks on passenger liners flying Allied flags actually constituted adequate justification for war. The spectrum of opinion included many different views, ranging from those of devout pacifists at one extreme to outright interventionists at the other. In the middle was a large group described by Wilson as demanding "two inconsistent things, firmness and the avoidance of war."

This was a confusing situation for a President who liked to be at the head of public opinion. Early in 1916, at the height of the spy and sabotage revelations, Wilson feared a swing toward chauvinism that would make it hard for him, in the next submarine crisis, to be as patient as in the past. He exclaimed to his private secretary, Joseph P. Tumulty: "If my reëlection as President depends upon my getting into war, I don't want to be President. . . . I intend to stand by the record I have made in all these cases, and take whatever action may be necessary, but I will not be rushed into war. . . ."

Only a few weeks later the pendulum had swung to the other extreme, at least in Congress. Thomas P. Gore, the blind senator from Oklahoma, and Representative Jeff McLemore of Texas proposed that American citizens be required to stay off armed belligerent ships. Wilson fought these resolutions on the ground that their passage would undermine him in his dealings with Germany. After a bitter fight with members of his own party, he was able to whip enough votes into line to defeat the resolutions.

Again there was a shift in public opinion. During the *Sussex* crisis, which followed hard on the heels of the legislative fight, the loudest voices Wilson heard were advocating a tougher policy toward Germany. Loudest of all was that of the man whom he had beaten for the presidency in 1912, Theodore Roosevelt. Wilson expected an increasing volume of criticism as the presidential election drew closer. To meet these attacks, he planned to have the Democrats adopt a platform emphasizing the New Freedom.

"Equal Suffrage" is the mocking title of this antisuffragette cartoon. The second Mrs. Wilson found the lady crusaders "disgusting creatures." She criticized her husband's address to their convention as "the only speech of my Precious One that I ever failed to enjoy, but I hated the subject so it was acute agony." She added sourly, "I had orchids from the suffragettes. . . ."

But when the convention met a strange thing happened. The keynote speaker, ex-Governor Martin Glynn of New York, began to extol Wilson's success in maintaining neutrality. The prepared text reviewed historical precedents for Wilson's actions against Germany, and after describing a similarly serious situation during President Grant's Administration, Glynn concluded: "But we didn't go to war." The delegates broke into furious applause. Responding to their mood, Glynn improvised other examples, ending each time with the selfsame sentence. Before he was through, the crowd was in near delirium. Democratic strategists were convinced that the winning slogan for Wilson's campaign was, "He kept us out of war."

Wilson never used this slogan himself. Always emphasizing that he had kept "peace with honor," he implied that peace would not necessarily be preserved if honor were the price. But to many people he was the peace candidate and his Republican opponent, Supreme Court Justice Charles Evans Hughes—who had the loud backing of Theodore Roosevelt—was the war candidate.

At the same time, the Democrats accused Hughes of courting the German-American vote. If there were real differences between Wilson and Hughes on issues of foreign policy, they are not apparent. Nevertheless, when Wilson learned of his hairbreadth triumph, he knew that many of the millions who voted for him had done so trusting that he would keep them out of war.

This knowledge oppressed him. The dominant note in his private correspondence in the months after re-election was anxiety, not jubilation. He felt that he had committed American prestige to his position on submarine warfare. If he backed down, the country might not again for a generation enjoy the respect of other nations. Yet a large number of the people clearly wanted him to retreat if the consequence of strict adherence to principle, in the inevitable crises that lay ahead, were to be war.

F ACING the grim prospects that confronted him after re-election, Wilson knew there was little hope of arranging acceptable peace proposals with the Allies. Robert Lansing, who had succeeded Bryan as Secretary of State, warned that overtures for peace carried the risk of an unacceptable answer from the Allies—one that might end with the United States on the side of the Germans. This risk became all the more apparent when, on December 12, 1916, Chancellor Bethmann-Hollweg surprised the world by declaring that Germany was ready to discuss terms with the Allies. Nevertheless Wilson strove to make peace, for he saw no other way to avoid the imminent danger of war over the submarine issue.

On December 18 he sent a note to all the belligerents asking them to reveal, in confidence, their conditions for peace. Despite their chancellor's recent speech, the Germans gave him a vague and disappointing answer. The Allies, on the other hand, returned a full and seemingly precise statement.

At the time of the 1916 election the German-American was often pictured as a dachshund with divided loyalties (above). Although the cartoon below accuses both Wilson and Republican candidate Charles Evans Hughes of courting the "hyphen" vote, Wilson repudiated it. Hughes lost votes in this group because Roosevelt, who spoke for him, blasted Germany.

In an effort to secure greater co-operation by Germany, Wilson went before Congress on January 22, 1917, and delivered a speech addressed as much to Germany as to America. He called for a settlement of all international issues, limitation of armaments, the opening of the seas to all nations and a world in which justice and friendly relations would prevail. And he promised that the United States would join other nations in guaranteeing peace if it were "a peace without victory."

Victory, however, was precisely what both sets of combatants still wanted.

Allied statesmen privately expressed scorn of Wilson for not realizing that the defeat and humiliation of Germany must precede lasting peace. On January 31 the Germans disclosed their minimum terms. These included annexation of parts of France and Russia, a protectorate over Belgium, colonial gains and reparations. On the same day Germany also stated that, in pursuing victory, unrestricted submarine warfare would be launched.

Many Americans at first doubted the authenticity of the notorious Zimmermann telegram. When Foreign Minister Zimmermann was asked to comment, a U.S. newsman (secretly in the pay of Germany) prompted: "Of course Your Excellency will deny this story." Zimmermann, perhaps remembering Washington's cherry tree, replied: "I cannot deny it. It is true."

FOR nearly two years Bethmann-Hollweg had been able to restrain those who insisted that the submarine could win the war regardless of American intervention. But in the late summer of 1916 the kaiser, despairing of victory, had summoned Field Marshal Paul von Hindenburg and his chief of staff, General Erich Ludendorff, to take the supreme command. Equally at the end of its rope, the Reichstag helped to vest the two officers with virtually dictatorial powers, including explicitly that of deciding whether or not to embark on an all-out submarine campaign. In early January 1917 Hindenburg and Ludendorff decided to take this step and to let the United States decide whether or not this meant war. The kaiser and the parliamentary leaders backed them up, and Bethmann-Hollweg was helpless.

By the last day of the month the submarines were on station, ready to begin the new campaign, and on that day the American government was notified that within 24 hours any and all shipping in the war zone, neutral vessels included, would be treated as fair game. Wilson felt he had to carry out the threat he had made during the *Sussex* crisis. On February 3 he announced to Congress that he had severed diplomatic relations. He added, however, that he could not believe Germany would actually carry out such a ruthless and reckless campaign: "Only actual overt acts on their part can make me believe it even now."

During succeeding weeks he tried, and failed, to persuade the German government that it should back down as it had in the past. On February 25 the British passenger liner *Laconia* was sunk with three Americans among those lost. On March 12 an American merchantman, the *Algonquin*, went down, followed within days by three other American vessels, *City of Memphis*, *Illinois* and *Vigilancia*. The Germans had supplied the overt acts.

Compounding the shock was the revelation that the German government had opened negotiations for an alliance with Mexico. A message from German Foreign Minister Arthur Zimmermann to the German minister in Mexico City had been intercepted and deciphered by the British and passed on via Ambassador Page to Washington. Dated January 16, it proposed that if the United States entered the war, Mexico should ally itself with Germany "on the following basis: make war together, make peace together, generous financial support and an understanding on our part that Mexico is to reconquer the lost territory in Texas, New Mexico, and Arizona."

When Wilson saw this text, his first reaction was indignation. When he learned that it had been sent through Washington over cable facilities which the State Department had specially opened to the German Embassy for possible communications about peace negotiations, he exclaimed, "Good Lord! Good Lord!" After the message was given to the press and its authenticity confirmed, war seemed to become a certainty.

Wilson was still not sure. And, as Winston Churchill was to recall when writing his history of World War I, the "action of the United States . . .

depended . . . upon the workings of this man's mind and spirit to the exclusion of almost every other factor." On the day after he received the Zimmermann text, Wilson proposed to Congress that American merchantmen be armed and authorized to fight submarines and that he be given broad authority to respond to Germany's challenge. Wilson hoped this measure might preserve America's honor without resort to all-out war.

But this was not to be. Pacifists and isolationists led by Senator La Follette blocked action with a filibuster. Although 75 of the 96 senators announced that they would vote for the bill if they could, La Follette's ranks held and the measure died. Then Wilson cried that a "little group of willful men, representing no opinion but their own, have rendered the great Government of the United States helpless and contemptible." He soon took matters in his own hands and by executive order authorized the arming of merchantmen.

What went through his mind in the next few weeks no one knows. The actual divisions in public opinion were still sharp. Fervor for war was confined to a vocal and growing minority, but sentiment for peace remained powerful. The large majority of the people appeared willing simply to trust that the President would make the right decision; they were ready to follow him. Public opinion did not guide Wilson; he had to guide it.

Frank Cobb, a newspaperman who talked with Wilson when his travail was nearing its end, recorded: "For nights, he said, he'd been lying awake going over the whole situation; over the provocation given by Germany, over the probable feeling in the United States, over the consequences to the settlement and the world at large if we entered the mêlée. . . . He said . . . that he had tried every way he knew to avoid war . . . that if there were any possibility of avoiding war he wanted to try it. 'What else can I do?' he asked. 'Is there anything else I can do?'"

On April 2 Wilson asked a joint session of Congress to declare war. He had feared that war might put an end to the ideals voiced in his "peace without victory" address. In his war message, however, he still talked with the fervor of a missionary; he rose above a mere demand for revenge to the vision of a world made "safe for democracy."

When Congress voted on April 6, six senators and 50 representatives stood out against war. Among them were not only men with German-American constituencies but also La Follette, George Norris of Nebraska and others who represented major elements in the progressivism of the preceding decade. They stood out as spokesmen for the idea that America should keep to itself, perfect its own institutions, and have as little as possible to do with the world in which it lived. But they were few.

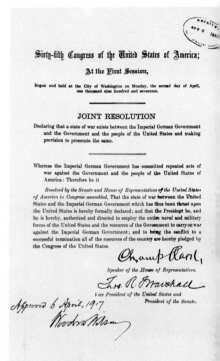

On April 1, 1917, as Wilson readied his message asking Congress to declare war (the joint resolution is above), "one thousand militant pacifists, each armed with a white tulip," prepared to go to Washington to protest. A critic jeered: "They are going to keep the nation out of war, and 14,000 other flower bearers from the rest of the United States are going to help them do it."

THE large majority in both houses voted enthusiastically for war, and when they did so, an epoch in American history came to a close. In the 1890s the United States had broken with its self-imposed isolation. Then, for a while, America had concentrated on its national concerns. But now it was isolated no more. Though men would later try once again to recapture the illusion of innocence and nonentanglement, the nation would from that day forward be a force, or at least a presence, in the affairs of all nations everywhere, and the presence of other nations would be felt in American affairs. The burden of power was on the country and could not be shaken loose. The Progressive Era had been the last in which the nation lived unto itself.

The secret heart of a stern man

DURING the second decade of the 20th Century the forces of liberal reform found a determined apostle in Thomas Woodrow Wilson. Son of a Presbyterian minister, Wilson placed all of his Calvinist zeal at the service of his crusades for progressive democracy. As president of Princeton, he turned a sleepy college into a great center of learning. As governor of New Jersey, he tamed his party's corrupt political machine. As 28th President of the United States, he pushed through Congress a comprehensive program of enlightened legislation. As a wartime leader, Wilson resolutely mobilized the country's might to win victory. But his ultimate goal—American participation in his cherished League of Nations—was tragically beyond his grasp.

The very qualities that gained him triumph also led to his defeat. His unruffled righteousness, his reluctance to compromise doomed him to break where others could bend. Yet within this fortress of pride, all but obscured by the public man, dwelt the devoted son, adoring husband and loving father. Below and on the following pages are excerpts (in italics) from his personal correspondence that reveal this Wilson. The photographs, taken by Nina Leen of LIFE, picture the important way stations on Wilson's journey to immortality.

And ah! what an unspeakable pleasure it is to me to think of what God has given me, my incomparable little wife and wonderful daughters.

THE CLOSE-KNIT FAMILY is seen at the fireside of their Princeton home in 1913. Even at the White House, the Wilsons were partial to quiet evenings together, reading aloud and singing.

The proper office of all books . . . is to stimulate the mind. The man who reads everything is like the man who eats everything; he can digest nothing.

A TREASURED BOOKCASE, bought with the first money Wilson earned, is seen at his birthplace in Staunton, Virginia. The scholar preferred the oil lamp long after electricity came in.

"Born and bred in a minister's family . . ."

FROM both sides of his family Wilson inherited a distinguished tradition of high intellectual achievement. His quiet, reserved mother came from a long line of learned Scottish churchmen. In later years Wilson would write of her to his wife that the "love of the best womanhood . . . entered my heart through those apronstrings." But it was his father who took charge of the boy's early education, transmitting the unquestioning faith that led Wilson to announce that "so far as religion is concerned, argument is adjourned." A stern disciplinarian who drilled young Tommy in reading, writing and rhetoric, the father showed boundless delight in his son's accomplishments. So lasting was his father's influence that Wilson, until he was past 40, did not make a major decision without first consulting him.

I bless God for my noble, strong, and saintly mother and for my incomparable father.

THE NURSERY of the manse at Staunton, Virginia, where Woodrow Wilson spent the first year of his life, before the family moved to Augusta, Georgia, contains his crib, a portrait of his mother, her vase with flowers in it and his father's favorite rocker.

I feel as though I ought to take off my shoes. This is holy ground. . . . I have never heard greater speaking in my life than I have heard from that rostrum.

THE CHAPEL of the Columbia Theological Seminary in South Carolina, which inspired the words above, is where Wilson at 16 accepted Christ, the prerequisite for formal church membership.

Do you remember the verses I gave you as we rode home from a picnic? I remember the charming blush with which you read them.

I have very decided tastes in ladies' dress.

THE SOCIAL ACTIVITY of the president of Princeton and his wife is indicated by the evening dress Mrs. Wilson made around 1902.

"The even, unbroken . . . perfection of my little wife."

IN 1883, while Wilson was languishing away at an uninspiring law practice in Atlanta, Georgia, he met Ellen Axson. Ellen's father, too, was a Presbyterian minister. She, like Wilson, had been reared in "a home of books and religion" and was well equipped to understand the lonely, ambitious youth who would soon become for her ". . . the greatest man in the world and the best." There were boat rides and buggy rides, walks and picnics in the countryside near Rome, Georgia, where Ellen lived. She introduced her suitor to Wordsworth and Browning. He disclosed an aspect of himself that was "personal, not current upon the vulgar tongue of the world." In 1885, shortly after he accepted the teaching post at Bryn Mawr that would lead him first to Wesleyan and then back to his beloved alma mater, Princeton, the couple was married. "My salvation is in being loved," he confessed. Ellen's capacity for loving, her patience and self-effacing loyalty completely fulfilled the needs of Wilson's temperament, and until her death 29 years later, his salvation was safe in her hands.

This whole affair is a <u>love</u> affair with me. . . . I want the house as <u>your</u> house—your framework and possession—your setting, and I shall work for it unremittingly from this time out.

THE PANTRY WINDOW in the house built when Wilson was a Princeton professor frames one of Mrs. Wilson's own paintings. The Wilson girls cherished a white cat named Puffins.

The popular professor

*I have had sight of the perfect place of learning in my thought:
a free place, and a various, where no man could be and not know
with how great a destiny knowledge had come into the world. . . . How can
a man who loves this place as I love it realize of a sudden that
he now has the liberty to devote every power that is in him to its service?*

AT PRINCETON, between 1890 and 1902, Wilson was "one of the most inspiring teachers a student ever had." His oratorical skill and wit as a lecturer breathed life into the dry facts of jurisprudence. His "questioning mind, . . . his preëminence in faculty debates," earned him the respect of his colleagues, his students and the alumni, and in 1902 Wilson was unanimously elected president of the university. With the move to "Prospect" (reflected in the pool in the photograph below), the official home of Princeton presidents, the era of professional scholarship was ended. The public man had begun to emerge.

The battle to reform
a university and a state

WE are not put into this world to sit still and know," Wilson said at his inauguration as president of Princeton. "We are put into it to act." And act he did—with sometimes disquieting speed. He revised the curriculum, attacked the anti-intellectual eating clubs, raised academic standards, introduced an advanced system of teaching and constructed seven new buildings. To those who accused him of changing too much too quickly in too arbitrary a manner, he answered that his chief concern was to bring about "an absolutely democratic rejuvenation in spirit." When Wilson lost the long, bitter battle over the location of the new graduate school and left to become governor of New Jersey in 1910, it was this same spirit that made him turn on the bosses who had supported him and attack their political aims. The "Presbyterian priest" promptly proved to be a remarkably practical "instrument of righteousness." To the astonishment of wary reformers, Wilson quickly charmed, chastened and cajoled the legislature into adopting within four months a host of enlightened measures.

*The trouble latent in my mind came out
in my dreams . . . the struggle . . .
with college foes, the sessions of hostile
trustees, the confused war of argument.*

THE CLEVELAND TOWER at the graduate college today stands where Dean West, Wilson's great antagonist, planned it—off the college campus. Wilson wanted it to be "at the heart of Princeton." But when an alumnus willed the university a large sum to be administered by West, Wilson gave up. "We have beaten the living," he told his wife. "But we cannot fight the dead."

*Every private comfort . . . is destroyed
and . . . one's life is made to turn
upon public affairs altogether. What
can be snatched from the public . . . one
can devote to his family or his friends.*

THE GOVERNOR'S OFFICE at Trenton is seen beyond his secretary's antechamber. The open doors indicate Wilson's early readiness to consult with all callers—reformers, petty politicians, labor leaders. It was here that he charmed some of his most implacable opponents into becoming his fanatical supporters —frequently in a single conference.

A grievous loss, a new love

THE death of Ellen Wilson in 1914, eighteen months after Wilson entered the White House, was a personal tragedy that tarnished the joy of his early success as a reform President. In the year that followed he "lived a lifetime of loneliness and heartache," while he persisted in his effort to stay out of the war in Europe.

But in 1915 Wilson fell in love with and married Edith Galt, a vivacious Virginia gentlewoman who gave him the same unstinting devotion that his first wife had offered. Together the happy couple played golf, went horseback riding, attended baseball games and vaudeville shows. In political affairs, too, she became his confidante, to the chagrin of some of his advisers. During the war Edith Wilson worked in a troop canteen and also helped decode messages. Later, during the sad days of illness and political defeat, she guarded her husband with such fierce determination that some even accused her of usurping his role. To Wilson, however, she was the person who showed him "the full meaning of life."

You are the only woman I know who can wear an orchid. Generally, it's the orchid that wears the woman. . . . A great . . . blessing has come to me . . . a lovely Washington woman . . . has promised to marry me.

THE FIRST LADY'S FUR PIECE, along with her hat, purse, necklace and other accessories, are seen much as she might have laid them out to be used for an evening of dining out or the theater.

I play golf every afternoon . . . while you are playing golf you <u>cannot</u> . . . be preoccupied with affairs. Each stroke . . . seems the most important thing in life.

GOLFING ENSEMBLE *(left)* includes Wilson's bag, balls, clubs and peaked cap. He kept up the sport at the suggestion of his physician, Dr. Cary Grayson, and played almost every day, in all kinds of weather, "sometimes as early as five in the morning."

Just a line with my own pen (this little machine is my pen) . . . I never stir from my key-board. I sit and . . . concentrate until the word comes.

WILSON'S TYPEWRITER is shown with his pince-nez. He had both with him on the West Coast tour in which he spoke up for the League of Nations. After using the machine at the White House, Wilson later brought it to his last residence in Washington.

"The machinery is worn out. . . . I am ready"

I am a sick man . . . but I am going to debate this issue with these gentlemen in their respective states whenever they come up for reelection if I have breath enough in my body to carry on . . .

In a last effort to win popular support for the Versailles Treaty and the League, the weary President delivered some 40 addresses on a three-week swing through the West in the fall of 1919. But on September 26, his health finally shattered, Wilson was rushed back to the capital where a stroke almost killed him. The night the Senate rejected the treaty, March 19, 1920, Wilson lay ill in the White House, his room lit far into the night *(right)*. Wilson turned to his physician and murmured: "Doctor, the devil is a busy man." His term ended, Wilson recovered sufficiently to move into a big house on S Street in Washington, where, on February 3, 1924, Wilson died in the copy of Lincoln's bed *(below)* made at his order.

CHRONOLOGY *A timetable of American and world events: 1901-1917*

WORLD EVENTS	EXPANSION and EXPLORATION	POLITICS	MILITARY and FOREIGN AFFAIRS	ECONOMICS and SCIENCE	THOUGHT and CULTURE
1901 Peking Agreement between China and the Great Powers ends Boxer Rebellion 1901 Wilhelm Röntgen wins Nobel Prize in Physics for discovery of X-rays; first year of Nobel awards 1902 Theodor Mommsen wins Nobel Prize in Literature 1903 and 1912 Renewals of Triple Alliance among Germany, Austria-Hungary and Italy 1903 Shaw's *Man and Superman* published 1903 Lumière brothers produce color photographic plates 1904 Première of Puccini's *Madame Butterfly* 1904 Entente Cordiale between France and Britain	1901 Five Civilized Tribes made U.S. citizens 1901 Supreme Court decides status of new possessions in Insular Cases 1901-10 8,795,386 immigrants enter the U.S. 1902 Reclamation Act sets aside proceeds from public land sales for irrigation projects 1902 Congress makes the Philippines unincorporated territory 1902 Creation of Crater Lake National Park 1903 First trans-Pacific cable completed	1901 McKinley assassinated, Theodore Roosevelt President 1901 Socialist Party of America organized 1902 Theodore Roosevelt pledges a "Square Deal" for both labor and industry 1902 Roosevelt mediation in anthracite-coal strike 1902-32 Oliver Wendell Holmes serves as justice of Supreme Court 1903 Elkins Act outlaws rebates, gives federal courts injunction power, defines unfair discrimination 1903 Creation of the Department of Commerce and Labor 1904 Theodore Roosevelt elected President	1901 Platt Amendment authorizes U.S. intervention in Cuba 1901 Army War College organized 1901 Capture of Aguinaldo, Filipino guerrilla leader 1902 Congress authorizes Panama Canal 1903 Panama secures independence, clearing way for building of Canal 1903 Army General Staff Corps created as part of War Department reorganization 1903 Alaskan boundary dispute with Canada settled 1904 Roosevelt Corollary defends U.S. intervention in the Western Hemisphere 1904-14 Construction of the Panama Canal	1901 Establishment of Rockefeller Institute for Medical Research 1901 Proof of transmission of yellow fever by mosquito offered by commission headed by Walter Reed 1901 Recognition of seriousness of disease caused by hookworm 1901-14 Agricultural expansion and prosperity 1902 First U.S. patent for production of rayon 1903 First successful heavier-than-air flight by Wright brothers 1903 Ford Motor Company organized 1904 Northern Securities Company ordered to dissolve 1904 National Association for Study and Prevention of Tuberculosis founded 1904 Formation of Bethlehem Steel Corporation 1904 National Child Labor Committee established 1904 Mount Wilson Observatory opened	1901 Connecticut passes first state law regulating auto speed and registration 1901 Pan-American Exposition at Buffalo 1901 Frank Norris' *The Octopus* published 1902 First Tournament of Roses football game in Pasadena 1902-12 Era of muckraking journalism 1903 Helen Keller's autobiography published 1903 *The Great Train Robbery*, first story-telling movie, exhibited 1903 Henry James's *The Ambassadors* published 1903 Jack London's *The Call of the Wild* published 1903 Debut of Enrico Caruso at the Metropolitan Opera 1904 Lincoln Steffens' *The Shame of the Cities* published 1904 onward John Dewey joins Columbia University faculty, exerting great influence on progressive education

1905 Pattern for Progressivism

WORLD EVENTS	EXPANSION and EXPLORATION	POLITICS	MILITARY and FOREIGN AFFAIRS	ECONOMICS and SCIENCE	THOUGHT and CULTURE
1905 Russian workers' revolt brings attempts at reform 1905 Separation of church and state in France 1906 Launching of H.M.S. *Dreadnought* intensifies Anglo-German naval race 1907 Second Hague Peace Conference 1907 Rudyard Kipling wins Nobel Prize in Literature 1907 Anglo-Russian agreement completes Triple Entente 1908 Austria annexes Bosnia and Herzegovina 1909 Blériot makes first airplane flight across English Channel 1909-34 Albert I king of the Belgians 1910 Cubist art movement takes shape 1910 *Psychoanalysis* by Sigmund Freud published 1910-36 George V king of England	1906 Creation of Mesa Verde National Park 1906 Forest Reserve Homestead Act 1907 Inland Waterways Commission created 1907 Oklahoma statehood 1907 Grazing interests oppose forest conservation policy 1907 All-time record for one year's immigration: 1,285,349 1908 National Conservation Commission formed 1909 320-acre land grants permitted in arid areas 1909 Peary reaches North Pole 1910 Census shows 91,972,266 inhabitants 1910 Creation of Glacier National Park	1905 Justice Holmes writes powerful dissent against invalidation of New York maximum-hours law 1905 Formation of the Industrial Workers of the World 1905-06 Robert M. La Follette elected U.S. senator but delays taking office to complete his Wisconsin reforms as a pattern for U.S. progressivism 1906 Oscar S. Straus becomes Secretary of Commerce and Labor, first Jewish Cabinet member 1907 Campaign contributions by corporations forbidden by law to candidates for national office 1908 Supreme Court hands down decisions unfavorable to labor unions 1908 William Howard Taft elected President 1909 Progressive Republicans in Congress take insurgent position 1909-11 Ballinger-Pinchot conservation controversy 1910 Mann Act declares white slavery illegal 1910 Elections return a Democratic majority in the House 1910 Roosevelt's progressive speeches at Osawatomie and Denver put him in opposition to Taft 1910-21 Edward D. White serves as Chief Justice of U.S.	1906 Roosevelt wins Nobel Peace Prize for mediation of Russo-Japanese War 1906 Roosevelt helps bring about Algeciras settlement of Moroccan crisis 1906-09 Provisional governor and U.S. troops re-establish order in Cuba 1907 "Gentlemen's Agreement" restricts Japanese immigration 1907-09 Around-the-world cruise of the U.S. battle fleet 1908 Root-Takahira Agreement recognizes Japanese sphere in Manchuria, guarantees status quo elsewhere in Pacific, confirms Open Door policy 1908-09 Secretary of State Elihu Root concludes 25 arbitration treaties 1909 U.S. intervention in Nicaragua 1910 Final resolution of Newfoundland fisheries dispute 1910 First airplane takeoff from deck of warship	1906 Pure Food and Drug Act and Meat Inspection Act become law 1906 Earthquake and fire destroy or damage most of San Francisco 1907 Banking panic reveals flaws in currency and financial structure 1908 Ford introduces the Model T 1908 Supreme Court decision in Danbury Hatters' Case declares unions subject to antitrust injunctions 1909 Psychoanalysis advanced in U.S. by Freud and Jung lectures 1909-15 Thomas Hunt Morgan's fruit-fly experiments lead to significant discoveries in genetics 1910 "Taylorization," or scientific management, becomes a byword in American industry 1910 Reappearance of Halley's Comet 1910 Creation of Bureau of Mines	1905 First Rotary Club formed 1905 Première of David Belasco's play, *The Girl of the Golden West* 1906 Upton Sinclair's *The Jungle* published 1907 First Mother's Day celebration, in Philadelphia 1907 Walter Rauschenbusch's *Christianity and the Social Crisis*, manifesto of the Protestant Social Gospel movement, published 1907 Henry Adams' *The Education of Henry Adams* privately published 1907-09 Georgia, Oklahoma, Mississippi, North Carolina, Tennessee, Alabama enact "dry" laws 1908 Establishment of Federal Council of Churches of Christ in America 1908 Ashcan School of realistic American painting holds group show in New York City 1909 National Association for the Advancement of Colored People founded 1910 Boy Scouts of America founded 1910 Carnegie Endowment for International Peace established 1910 First Father's Day celebrated in Spokane 1910 onward Rise of the modern

1911–1913

1911 Agadir incident in Morocco
1911 Amundsen reaches South Pole
1911-12 Franco-Russian military agreement
1911-20 Mexican Revolution
1912 China becomes a republic
1912 French establish protectorate over Morocco
1912-13 Balkan Wars
1913 Rabindranath Tagore wins Nobel Prize in Literature

1911-20 5,735,811 immigrants enter the U.S.

1912 New Mexico and Arizona statehood
1913 Domestic parcel post begins
1913 Taft vetoes compulsory literacy test for immigrants

1911 Presidential commission recommends a national budget and administrative reforms
1911 National Progressive Republican League established
1911 Completion of Taft-Roosevelt split
1912 Roosevelt and Progressives bolt the Republican party, run third-party slate
1912 Socialist candidate Debs polls 900,672 votes
1912 Woodrow Wilson elected President
1913 Adoption of 16th Amendment (income tax) and 17th Amendment (direct election of senators)
1913 Department of Commerce and Labor divided into two separate Cabinet posts
1913 Interstate shipment of liquor into "dry" states prohibited
1913 Underwood Tariff reverses upward tariff trend

1911 North Pacific Sealing Convention to end slaughter of seals in open sea
1912-25 U.S. intervention in Nicaragua

1913-14 Bryan negotiates "cooling-off" treaties with 30 nations
1913-17 U.S. intervention in Mexican affairs

1911 Sperry gyrocompass patented
1911 Standard Oil of New Jersey ordered dissolved, American Tobacco Company forced to reorganize
1911 Triangle Shirtwaist factory fire tragedy brings New York safety legislation
1912 Violent textile strike at Lawrence, Massachusetts
1912-32 Dr. Harvey Cushing's research leads to notable advances in brain surgery
1913 Pujo Committee Report on financial concentration spurs creation of Federal Reserve System
1913 American College of Surgeons organized
1913 Coolidge X-ray tube developed
1913 Woolworth Building completed, until 1929 world's tallest building

1911 U.S. Roman Catholics have three cardinals for first time
1911 Carnegie Corporation established
1911 Irving Berlin's "Alexander's Ragtime Band" published
1911 Edith Wharton's *Ethan Frome* published
1912 Zane Grey's *Riders of the Purple Sage* published
1913 Armory Show of contemporary European and American Art
1913. Charles A. Beard's *An Economic Interpretation of the Constitution* published
1913 Rockefeller Foundation established to "promote the well-being of mankind throughout the world"
1913 Robert Frost's first book of poems, *A Boy's Will*, published in England
1913-16 Mack Sennett begins slapstick school of movie comedy

1914 The First World War

1914 Murder of Archduke Franz Ferdinand at Sarajevo
July-Aug. 1914 War breaks out in Europe
Sept. 1914 First battle of Marne halts initial German advance and begins prolonged trench warfare on Western Front
Feb. 1915 Germany begins first submarine campaign against merchantmen
April 22, 1915 Germans introduce use of poison gas
May 1915 Italy leaves Triple Alliance, joins the Allies
1915-16 German Zeppelins raid London
1915-16 Allied Dardanelles campaign ends in failure

1914 Panama Canal Zone gets permanent civil government
1915 Creation of Rocky Mountain National Park

1914 Clayton Antitrust Act
1915 La Follette's Seamen's Act improves living conditions and safety on ships

1914 U.S. proclaims neutrality in World War I
1914 Bryan-Chamorro Treaty for Nicaraguan canal
1915 *Lusitania* and *Arabic* sinkings bring strong notes from Wilson that result in modification of German unrestricted submarine warfare
1915 Robert Lansing succeeds Bryan as Secretary of State
1915 U.S. Coast Guard established
1915-16 Preparedness movement leads to National Defense Act, which expands Army to 175,000 and establishes ROTC
1915-17 Private U.S. investors lend Allies $2.3 billion

1914 American ships carry only 8 per cent of nation's exports
1914 Robert H. Goddard receives first U.S. patent for multistage rockets
1914 Smith-Lever Act provides federal aid for agricultural education
1914-20 Agricultural boom caused by war conditions
1915 Creation of the Federal Trade Commission
1915 U.S. Steel ruled not in violation of antitrust legislation
1915 Joseph Goldberger finds that pellagra is a deficiency disease

1914 Charles Chaplin first dons the outfit of a tramp
1914 Vachel Lindsay's *Congo and Other Poems* published
1914 Theodore Dreiser's *The Titan* published
1914 W. C. Handy's "St. Louis Blues" published
1914 Edgar Rice Burroughs publishes first Tarzan novel
1914 Joyce Kilmer's poem "Trees" published
1914 Walter Lippmann's *Drift and Mastery* published
1914 D. W. Griffith's movie *The Birth of a Nation* exhibited
1915 Revival of the Ku Klux Klan
1915 Edgar Lee Masters' *Spoon River Anthology* published

1916 "He Kept Us Out of War"

1916 Lloyd George forms coalition ministry
1916 Battle of Jutland
Feb.-Dec. 1916 Battle of Verdun
March 1917 February Revolution (by Russian calendar)
1917 Balfour Declaration on Palestine
1917 Mutinies in the French army reflect war weariness
1917 Germany resumes unrestricted submarine warfare
Nov. 1917 Bolsheviks seize power in Russia

1916 Jones Act promises Philippines eventual independence
1916 National Park Service founded
1916 Federal-Aid Road Act establishes federal aid program for state highway building
1917 U.S. purchases Virgin Islands from Denmark
1917 Puerto Ricans given U.S. citizenship
1917 Congress establishes literacy test for immigrants over presidential veto
1917 Creation of Mount McKinley National Park

1916 Federal Farm Loan Act, U.S. Warehouse Act
1916 Newton D. Baker becomes Secretary of War
1916 Adamson Act specifies eight-hour day on interstate railroads
1916 Woodrow Wilson re-elected President as his followers boast, "He kept us out of war"
1916-39 Louis D. Brandeis justice of Supreme Court
1917 Senate cloture rule permits two-thirds majority to limit debate

1916 Council of National Defense formed
1916 U.S. troops enter Mexico to counter Pancho Villa's raids
1916-24 American military occupation of Santo Domingo
1917 Wilson asks for "peace without victory"
1917 Zimmermann Note proposes alliance with Mexico against U.S.
1917 U.S. merchantmen armed
April 6, 1917 Declaration of War passed, signed by Wilson

1916 U.S. exports reach $5.4 billion, a record
1916 Creation of U.S. Shipping Board
1916 National Research Council created
1916-19 National debt jumps from $1.2 billion to $25.6 billion

1916 Eugene O'Neill's *Bound East for Cardiff* produced by Provincetown Players
1916 Edwin Arlington Robinson's *The Man Against the Sky* published
1916-17 First U.S. appearances of singer Amelita Galli-Curci and violinist Jascha Heifetz
1917 Inauguration of Pulitzer Prize awards
1917 Margaret Sanger jailed for conducting birth control clinic
1917 Society of Independent Artists organized as a protest against conservatism of National Academy of Design

FOR FURTHER READING

These books were selected for their interest and authority in the preparation of this volume, and for their usefulness to readers seeking additional information on specific points. An asterisk (*) marks works available in both hard-cover and paperback editions; a dagger (†) indicates availability only in paperback.

GENERAL READING

Bailey, Thomas A., *Diplomatic History of the American People.* Appleton-Century-Crofts. 1958.
*Beale, Howard Kennedy, *Theodore Roosevelt and the Rise of America to World Power.* Johns Hopkins Press, 1956.
Coleman. McAlister. *Men and Coal.* Farrar & Rinehart. 1943.
Dulles, Foster Rhea, *Labor in America.* Thomas Y. Crowell, 1961.
Faulkner, Harold, *Decline of Laissez Faire 1897-1917.* Rinehart, 1951.
*Filler, Louis, *Crusaders for American Liberalism.* Harcourt, Brace & World, 1939.
*Hofstadter, Richard, *The Age of Reform, from Bryan to F.D.R.* Knopf, 1955.
Holbrook, Stewart Hall, *Age of the Moguls.* Doubleday, 1953.
*Mowry, George E., *Era of Theodore Roosevelt, 1900-1912.* Harper & Brothers, 1958.
Roosevelt, Theodore, *An Autobiography.* Scribner's, 1946.
Yellen, Samuel, *American Labor Struggles.* Harcourt, Brace & World, 1936.

LORDS OF CREATION (CHAPTER 1)

*Allen, Frederick Lewis, *Great Pierpont Morgan.* Harper & Brothers, 1949.
†Dunne, Finley Peter, *The World of Mr. Dooley.* (Louis Filler, editor). Collier Books, 1962.
*Faulkner, Harold Underwood, *Politics, Reform and Expansion 1890-1900.* Harper & Brothers, 1959.
*Glackens, Ira, *William Glackens and the Ashcan Group.* Crown Publishers, 1957.
Hendrick, Burton J., *Life of Andrew Carnegie* (2 vols.). Doubleday, Doran, 1932.
Kennan, George M., *E. H. Harriman* (2 vols.). Houghton Mifflin, 1922.
La Follette, Suzanne, *Art in America.* Harper & Brothers, 1930.
McDonald, Forrest, *Insull.* University of Chicago Press, 1962.
Nevins, Allan, and Frank E. Hill, *Ford: The Times, the Man, the Company.* Scribner's, 1954.
Winkler, John K., *Tobacco Tycoon: Story of James Buchanan Duke.* Random House, 1942.
Woytinsky, W. S., and E. S. Woytinsky, *World Population and Production; Trends and Outlook.* Twentieth Century Fund, 1953.

THE OTHER HALF (CHAPTER 2)

Brody, David, *Steelworkers in America, the Nonunion Era.* Harvard University Press, 1960.
Chafee, Zachariah, *Free Speech in the United States.* Harvard University Press, 1941.
DeForest, Robert, and Lawrence Veiller, *Tenement House Problem* (2 vols.). Macmillan, 1903.
Egbert, Donald Drew, *Socialism and American Life.* Princeton University Press, 1952.
*Ginger, Raymond, *The Bending Cross.* Rutgers University Press, 1949.
Josephson, Matthew, *Sidney Hillman; Statesman of American Labor.* Doubleday, 1952.
Link, Arthur S., *American Epoch.* Knopf, 1955.
Rayback, Joseph G., *History of American Labor.* Macmillan, 1959.
*Riis, Jacob, *How the Other Half Lives.* Peter Smith, 1959.
Roberts, Peter, *Anthracite Coal Communities.* Macmillan, 1904.
Shannon, David, *Socialist Party of America: A History.* Macmillan, 1955.
Van Vorst, Bessie and Marie, *The Woman Who Toils.* Doubleday, Page, 1903.

PROGRESSIVISM AT THE GRASS ROOTS (CHAPTER 3)

Cramer, Clarence H., *Newton D. Baker.* World Publishing Company, 1961.
Faulkner, Harold, *Quest for Social Justice.* Macmillan, 1931.
La Follette, Belle and Fola, *Robert M. La Follette.* Macmillan, 1953.
*Pringle, Henry, *Theodore Roosevelt.* Harcourt, Brace & World, 1931.
Regier, C. C., *Era of the Muckrakers.* University of North Carolina Press, 1932.
Steffens, Lincoln, *Autobiography.* Harcourt, Brace & World, 1931.
*Swanberg, William A., *Citizen Hearst.* Scribner's, 1961.
White, W. A., *The Autobiography of William Allen White.* Macmillan, 1946.

THE SQUARE DEAL (CHAPTER 4)

*Blum, John Morton, *Republican Roosevelt.* Harvard University Press, 1954.
*Hofstadter, Richard, *American Political Tradition.* Knopf, 1948.
Morison, Elting E. (ed.), *Letters of Theodore Roosevelt* (6 vols.). Harvard University Press, 1951.
Ripley, William Z., *Railroads: Rates and Regulation.* Longmans, Green, 1912.
Stephenson, Nathaniel Wright, *Nelson W. Aldrich; a Leader in American Politics.* Scribner's, 1930.
Sullivan, Mark, *Our Times* (Vol. II). Scribner's, 1927.
Tarbell, Ida, *History of the Standard Oil Company* (Vol. II). Macmillan, 1925.
Wagenknecht, Edward C., *Seven Worlds of Theodore Roosevelt.* Longmans, Green, 1958.

THE TRIUMPH OF PROGRESSIVISM (CHAPTER 5)

Bolles, Edmund Blaire, *Tyrant from Illinois; Uncle Joe Cannon's Experiment with Personal Power.* Norton, 1951.
Coyle, David, *Conservation: An American Story of Conflict and Accomplishment.* Rutgers University Press, 1957.
*Harbaugh, William Henry, *Power and Responsibility; the Life and Times of Theodore Roosevelt.* Farrar, Straus, 1961.
Link, Arthur S., *The New Freedom.* Princeton University Press, 1956.
Lowitt, Richard, *George W. Norris; the Making of a Progressive.* Syracuse University Press, 1963.
Mason, Alpheus, *Bureaucracy Convicts Itself.* Princeton University Press, 1941.
*Mowry, George E., *Theodore Roosevelt and the Progressive Movement.* University of Wisconsin Press, 1946.
Pinchot, Gifford, *Breaking New Ground.* Harcourt, Brace & World, 1947.
Pringle, Henry F., *Life and Times of William Howard Taft.* Farrar & Rinehart, 1939.
Satterlee, Herbert, *J. Pierpont Morgan, an Intimate Portrait.* Macmillan, 1939.

THE BIG STICK (CHAPTER 6)

Bemis, Samuel Flagg, *Diplomatic History of the United States.* Holt, 1955.
Jessup, Philip, *Elihu Root* (2 vols.). Dodd, 1938.
Leech, Margaret, *In the Days of McKinley.* Harper, 1959.
Livezey, William Edmund, *Mahan on Sea Power.* University of Oklahoma Press, 1947.
Mack, Gerstle, *The Land Divided.* Knopf, 1944.
Mitchell, Donald, *History of the Modern American Navy.* Knopf, 1946.
*Perkins, Dexter, *History of the Monroe Doctrine.* Little, Brown, 1955.
Pratt, Julius, *History of the United States Foreign Policy.* Prentice-Hall, 1955.
Zabriskie, Edward H., *American-Russian Rivalry in the Far East.* University of Pennsylvania Press, 1946.

THE ROAD TO WAR (CHAPTER 7)

Baker, Ray Stannard, *Life and Letters of Woodrow Wilson* (2 vols.). Doubleday, 1927.
Bell, H.C.F., *Woodrow Wilson and the People.* Doubleday, 1945.
*Blum, John Morton, *Woodrow Wilson and the Politics of Morality.* Little, Brown, 1956.
Garraty, John A., *Woodrow Wilson; a Great Life in Brief.* Knopf, 1956.
Link, Arthur S., *Wilson: The Road to the White House.* Princeton University Press, 1947.
Link, Arthur S., *The Struggle for Neutrality, 1914-1915.* Princeton University Press, 1960.
McAdoo, Eleanor Wilson (ed.), *The Priceless Gift, [their] Love Letters.* McGraw-Hill, 1962.
Seymour, Charles (ed.), *The Intimate Papers of Colonel House.* Houghton Mifflin, 1926.
Walworth, Arthur, *Woodrow Wilson: World Prophet* (2 vols.). Longmans, Green, 1958.

ACKNOWLEDGMENTS

The editors of this book are particularly indebted to the following persons and institutions for their assistance in the preparation of this volume: Charles Forcey, Associate Professor of History, Rutgers University, New Brunswick, New Jersey; Mrs. Julie C. Herzog, The Woodrow Wilson Foundation, New York City; Mrs. Elsie M. Peters and Mrs. Herbert McK. Smith, The Woodrow Wilson Birthplace, Staunton, Virginia; Wilson Dozier, Staunton, Virginia; James A. Elrod Jr., Rome, Georgia; Ira Daniels, Office of the Governor, Trenton, New Jersey; Robert Stewart and Mrs. Ruby Stefansson, National Trust for Historic Preservation, Washington, D.C.; Edmund DeLong and Mr. and Mrs. John W. Ballantine, Princeton, New Jersey; Roy Flynn, Winthrop College, Rock Hill, South Carolina; Mrs. Margaret B. Klapthor, Smithsonian Institution, Washington, D.C.; The White House; Mrs. Richard Derby and Mr. and Mrs. William Johnston, Oyster Bay, New York; Mrs. Virginia Gray, Duke University, Durham, North Carolina; Helen MacLachlan, Theodore Roosevelt Association, New York City; Mrs. Irene Watson, AFL-CIO, Washington, D.C.; I. Warshaw, New York City; Sol Novin, Culver Pictures Inc., New York City; Roberts Jackson, Bettmann Archive, New York City; Carl Stange, Library of Congress, Washington, D.C.; Professor Charles Neu, Rice University, Houston, Texas; Henry E. Edmunds, Ford Motor Company, Dearborn, Michigan; Mrs. Sheila Ford and Robert Haynes, Harvard College Library, Cambridge, Massachusetts; Louise Stoops, United States Steel Company, New York City; Mrs. John Sloan, New York City; William Clutz, Museum of Modern Art, New York City; Sam Pearce, Museum of the City of New York; Bartlett H. Hayes Jr., Addison Gallery of American Art, Andover, Massachusetts; and Judy Higgins. The author, for his part, wishes to thank Alan Rau, Paul Boyer, Mrs. Frederick Burnham and Catherine Herrlich.

PICTURE CREDITS

The sources for the illustrations in this book are shown below. Credits for pictures from left to right are separated by semicolons, top to bottom by dashes. Sources have been abbreviated as follows: Bettmann—Bettmann Archive; Brown—Brown Brothers; Culver—Culver Pictures; LC—Library of Congress; N-YHS— The New-York Historical Society, N.Y.C.; NYPL—The New York Public Library

CHAPTER 1: 6—Eric Schaal, courtesy a private collection. 8—Courtesy the New York *Times.* 9—Culver—Bettmann. 10, 11—Ford Motor Company except left Wide World Photos. 13—NYPL. 14, 15—Bettmann; Culver. 16, 17—NYPL. 18, 19—John Sloan: *Memory,* 1906, etching. Philadelphia Museum of Art; Fernand Bourges, courtesy Mr. and Mrs. Arthur G. Altschul. 20, 21—Addison Gallery of American Art, Phillips Academy, Andover, Mass. except bottom right Fernand Bourges, collection of the Memorial Art Gallery of the University of Rochester. 22, 23—Herbert Orth, collection of Mr. and Mrs. Meyer P. Potamkin; William Glackens: *Hammerstein's Roof Garden.* c. 1901. Collection of the Whitney Museum of American Art, New York—Robert S. Crandall, courtesy Museum of Fine Arts, Boston. 24, 25—Herbert Orth, courtesy the Estate of John Sloan. 26, 27—Herbert Orth, the White House Collection. 28, 29—Henry B. Beville, courtesy Phillips Gallery, Washington—Eric Schaal, courtesy Henry Pearlman Foundation; Fernand Bourges, courtesy Mr. and Mrs. Arthur G. Altschul.

CHAPTER 2: 30—J. R. Eyerman, courtesy Los Angeles County Museum. 32, 33—George Eastman House Collection; Brown. 34—Reproduced by permission. 35—Culver—Brown. 36 through 39—Culver. 40, 41—Culver; Brown. 42, 43—George P. West, *Report on Ludlow,* 1914 (The National Archives) except right Culver. 44, 45—Culver. 46, 47—United Press International; Underwood & Underwood—Duke University Library (2). 48, 49—Culver; Brown.

CHAPTER 3: 50—Arthur Siegel, courtesy The Pugsley Union at South Dakota State College, Brookings, S.D. 52, 53—Culver; Bettmann. 54, 55—Culver; United Press International. 56, 57—Brown except top left Free Lance Photographers Guild. 58, 59—Culver except right NYPL. 60, 61—Bettmann; Eric Schaal, courtesy Museum of the City of New York. 62, 63—Culver; Museum of the City of New York; Brown—Brown; Culver. 64, 65—Left: Warshaw Collection of Business Americana—Brown; right: The Museum of Modern Art Film Library. 66, 67—Warshaw Collection of Business Americana except top left Brown. 68, 69—Brown; John Mulholland Collection; Culver; The Museum of Modern Art Film Library.

CHAPTER 4: 70—Courtesy of The White House. 72, 73—NYPL; N-YHS. 74, 75—Bettmann (2)—Culver (2). 76, 77—General Dynamics Corporation; Brown. 78—This letter from Theodore Roosevelt is reprinted with the permission of Charles Scribner's Sons from *Theodore Roosevelt's Letters to his Children,* edited by Joseph Bucklin Bishop. Copyright 1919 Charles Scribner's Sons; renewal copyright 1947 Edith K. Carow Roosevelt. 79—Theodore Roosevelt Collection, Harvard College Library—Courtesy LC. 80, 81—Theodore Roosevelt Association; Bettmann—Culver. 82, 83—Brown; Eric Schaal, TIME cover by Aaron Bohrod. 84, 85—Left: Theodore Roosevelt Association; right: Culver *New York Herald Tribune;* Theodore Roosevelt Collection, Harvard College Library. 86, 87—Underwood & Underwood; Free Lance Photographers Guild; Wide World Photos; Brown; Free Lance Photographers Guild; Brown—N-YHS (2). 88, 89—Left: Underwood & Underwood; right: Theodore Roosevelt Association (2)—courtesy Mrs. Richard Derby; Theodore Roosevelt Collection, Harvard College Library—courtesy Mrs. Theodore Roosevelt. 90, 91—United Press International except left *Harper's Weekly.* 92, 93—Theodore Roosevelt Association; Gottscho-Schleisner.

CHAPTER 5: 94—Courtesy of The White House. 96—Culver. 98, 99—Brown. 101—by A. B. Walker in LIFE. 102, 103—From *The Evening Sun,* Baltimore; Culver. 104, 105—Brown; Culver. 106, 107—Culver; Salt River Project, Phoenix. 108—Laurence Lowry from Rapho Guillumette. 109—Thomas E. Benner from Shostal—Dmitri Kessel. 110, 111—Ansel Adams from Magnum. 112—Joern Gerdts. 113—Joern Gerdts; N. R. Farbman. 114—Eliot Elisofon, TIME-LIFE Picture Agency, (c) 1972 Time Incorporated. 115—N. R. Farbman. 116, 117—Russ Kinne from Photo Researchers, Inc. except top right Sven Gillsäter.

CHAPTER 6: 118—The Metropolitan Museum of Art, Arthur H. Hearn Fund, 1935 courtesy American Heritage Publishing Co., Inc. 121—Bettmann. 122, 123—Bettmann; Brown. 124, 125—Culver; from the collection of Douglas P. Ball. 126 through 129—Culver. 130, 131—Collection of Lorraine Dexter courtesy American Heritage Publishing Co., Inc.; Bettmann. 132, 133—Courtesy of Automobile Manufacturers Association; Culver—Photographed at Henry Ford Museum and Greenfield Village, Dearborn, Michigan. 134, 135—Warshaw Collection of Business Americana. 136—Arnold Genthe, LC Collection, copied by Robert Kafka except right Paul Guillumette from Rapho Guillumette, copied by Robert Kafka. 137—Courtesy Georgia O'Keeffe for Alfred Stieglitz Estate, copied by Robert Kafka. 138, 139—Culver except left Brown.

CHAPTER 7: 140—Courtesy of The White House. 142, 143—NYPL; Bettmann. 145—Culver. 146, 147—Top right: Culver—Brown; The American Numismatic Society. 148, 149—Brown; Culver. 152, 153—Culver; Brown. 154, 155—Underwood & Underwood; Nina Leen. 156, 157—Nina Leen; Nina Leen, courtesy Winthrop College, the South Carolina State College for Women, Rock Hill, S.C. 158—Nina Leen. 159—Nina Leen, courtesy The Woodrow Wilson Foundation. 160 through 167—Nina Leen.

INDEX

*This symbol in front of a page number indicates a photograph or painting of the subject mentioned.